The Registers of Monk Fryston: In the West Riding of Yorkshire: 1538-1678

Eng Parish Monk Fryston

THE

Registers

OF

Monk Fryston,

IN THE

WEST RIDING OF YORKSHIRE.

Issued by
THE PARISH REGISTER SOCIETY.

(V.)

ters

'STON,

YORKSHIRE:

ß.

RTH.

REGISTER SOCIETY.

The Registers

OF

MONK FRYSTON,

IN THE WEST RIDING OF YORKSHIRE:

1538—1678.

TRANSCRIBED BY

(THE LATE)

J. D. HEMSWORTH.

Contents:

LONDON:

ISSUED TO SUBSCRIBERS BY THE PARISH REGISTER SOCIETY.

1896.

PREFACE.

The Registers of Monk Fryston to 1812 consist of eight volumes; Vol. I. now printed, contains entries of Baptisms, Burials, and Marriages from 1538 to 1678, which were transcribed by the late J. D. Hemsworth, Esq.

The succeeding volumes are now being transcribed, and will appear in a subsequent volume of The Parish Register Society's Publications.

In Memoriam.

John David Hemsworth.

This gentleman was the younger son of Benjamin Hemsworth, of Monk Fryston Hall, by Elisabeth his wife, the only surviving child and heiress of John Bower of Smeathalls.

He was born 4 May, 1851, and was educated at Harrow and Caius College, Cambridge, where he graduated and entered his Name as a Student of the Temple. He took great interest in the Restoration of Monk Fryston Church, to which he gave the Organ. He transcribed this Register and collated the proofs, but died while the sheets were in the press, on 18 February, 1895.

R. E. H. Duke.

The Parsonage,
   Monk Fryston,
     March,
       A.D. 1896.

MONCK FRIESTON PARISH.

———•———

The book conteyning all the weddings Christenings and Burialls within the Parish of Monck frieston from the ffirst day of December which was in the yere of our Lord God 1538 And in the yere of the Reign of our Soveraine Lord King Henry the Eight the xxx^th written by Peter Marshall then Curate there as followeth, viz :

December, 1538.

C. Imprimis Isabell Parker christened the iiij^th day.
B. Itm. Agnes Parker buried the ffift day.
C. Itm. Jenet Baker christened the vj^th day.
C. Itm. Eline ffairebie christened the xxix^th day.

Januarie.

C. Itm. Will'm Collingwoorth christened the xv^th day.
C. Itm. Jenet ffoyster christened the said xv^th day.
B. Itm. the said Jenet buried the xvj^th day.
C. Itm. Anthonie Nelson christened the xxiij^th day.

ffebruarius vacat.

Marche, 1539.

C. Itm. Jenet Turpin christened the xxviij^th day.

Aprill.

B. Itm. Thomas Richardson buried the vj^th day.
B. Itm. Grace Hamond buried the ix^th day.
B. Itm. Oswald ffederstonhauth buried the xiij^th day.
B. Itm. John Hamond buried the xxviij^th day.
C. Itm. Elizabeth Taylor christened the last day.

May.

C. Itm. John Bradford christened the xviij^th day.

June.

B. Itm. Jenet Berredge buried the ffirst day.
C. Itm. John Marshall christened the xvj^th day.
B. Itm. John Whitley buried the xviij^th day.

Julie.

B. John Marshall buried the . . . .

August.

B. Itm. Xp̄ofer Kendall buried third day.
C. Itm. Katheren Norman christened the iiij^th day.
C. Itm. Jenet Rayner christened the ix^th day.
C. Itm. Miles Tompson christened the xxj^th day.

I

September.

B.   Itm. Uxor Nelson buried the eight day.
C.   Itm. Jenet Shippen christened the xxij[th] day.

October.

M.   Itm. Richard Biwater & Mary hallile married the fift day.
B.   Itm. John . . . . . buried the vij[th] day.
M.   Itm. Roger Pearson and Jenet Harrison were married the xix[th] day.
B.   Itm. Margaret Walker buried the xxiiij[th] day.
C.   Itm. John Johnson christened the xxix[th] day.

November.

M.   Itm. John Youle and Isabell Robinson were married the xj[th] day.
M.   Itm. John Sikes and Katheren Dawson were married the xxij[th] day.
M.   Itm. Will'm Griesdail and Agnes Richardson were married the xxiiij[th] day.

December, 1539.

B.   Itm. Will'm hay buried the xxviij[th] day.

Januarie.

C.   Itm. Margaret Scot christened the xij[th] day.
C.   Itm. Will'm Watkin christened the xxj[th] day.
B.   Itm. Raulph Roundail buried the xxij[th] day.

Februarie.

C.   Itm. Will'm Hay christened the ix[th] day.
C.   Itm. Jenet ffuster christened the xxiiij[th] day.
B.   Itm. John Simpull buried the xxvij[th] day.
C.   Itm. Henry Huscroft christened the last day.

March.

B.   Itm. ffraunces Browne buried the second day.

Aprill, 1540.

C.   Itm. Alice Berredge christened the xxiij[th] day.
C.   Itm. Will'm Gilliam christened the xxiiij[th] day.
C.   Itm. Will'm Metthay christened the xxvj[th] day.

                      Maius vacat.

June.

B.   Itm. Margaret Joy buried the xj[th] day.

Julie.

B.   Will'm Metthay buried the xxx day.

August.

B.   Itm. Jenet ffurth buried the xj[th] day.
B.   Itm. Anthony Dawson buried the xiiij[th] day.
C.   Itm. Isabell Carnabie christened the xv day.
C.   Itm. Robert Griesley christened the xv day.
B.   Itm. Will'm Wilson buried the xvj day.
C.   Itm. Alice Dice christened the xxv[th] day.
B.   Itm. Will'm Nelson buried the xxvj[th] day.

September.

B.   Itm. John ffurth buried the xth day.
B.   Itm. Rob'rt Shippen buried the xv[th] day.
      Itm. Jenet Ward christene[d] the xxj[th] day.

October.

3. Itm. John Smithe buried the xvj day.
2. Itm. Katheren Pearson christened the xvij day.

November.

3. Itm. Mr John Medley buried the ij day.
3. Itm. Margaret Hamond buried the xx^th day.
2. Itm. Cecelie Bank christened the xxij day.

December.

3. Itm. Jenet Baker buried the xth day.
2. Itm. Agnes Staynton xpned the xxvj^th day.

Januarie.

2. Itm. John Nelson xpned the ij day.
2. Itm. Thomas Nelson christened the xth day.
3. John Wilson buried the xiij day.
2. Itm. Isabell Burro christened the xv day.
2. Itm. Alice Nut christened the xvj . . . .
2. Itm. Margaret Baker christened the xxij^th day.
4. Itm. John Sykes and Alison Nelson married the xxiiij day.
3. Itm. Isabell Burro buried the same day.
2. Itm. M'gery ffurth christened the xxix^th day.
4. Itm. John Wise and Isabell Shippen married the xxx^th day.

Februarie.

4. Itm. Robert Cooper and Jenet Olred married the vj^th day.
2. Itm. Edward Tompson christened the xxvj^th day.

March.

3. Itm. Margaret Smith buried the xix^th day.
3. Itm. John Nelson buried the xxv^th day.

April vacat.

May, 1541.

3. Itm. Agnes Walker buried the ij day.

June.

2. Itm. Thomas Shippen christened the xiiij^th day.
2. Itm. Thomas Sampull christened the said day.
2. Itm. Jenet Brown xpned the xxvj^th day of July.
4. Itm. John Watson & Jenet Barmbow married xiiij day August.

September.

3. Itm. Jenet Gibson buried the viij^th day.
2. Itm. John Wise christened the xiij^th day.
3. Itm. Agnes Tutill buried the xv^th day.
2. Itm. John Watkin christened the xviij^th day.
2. Itm. Elinore Butter christened the xxvj^th day.

October vacat.

November.

2. Itm. Alice Wells christened xj day.
2. Itm. John Smith christened the xij^th day.
3. Itm. Jenet Brown buried the xxv^th day.

December vacat.

Januarie.

M. Itm. Henry Brown & Isabell Turpin married the xxij day.
C. Itm. Agnes Pearson christened the xxvj^th day.
C. Itm. Katteron Cowper christened the xxviij^th day.

Februarie.

C. Itm. Richard Gilliam christened the viij^th day.
C. Itm. Persevall Collingwoorth xpned the xth day.
C. Itm. Henry Brogden xpned the xiiij^th day.
C. Itm. ffraunc Nelson xpned the xvj^th day.
                                    Martius vac.

April, 1542.

C. Itm. Will'm Marshall christened the iij^th day.

May.

C. Itm. Will'm Nelson christened the xv^th day.
C. Itm. John Browne christened the xvj day.
                                    Junius vac.

Julie.

C. Itm. Will'm Mettham christened the iij day.
C. Itm. An Turpin christened the xxiij^th day.
C. Itm. An Berredge xpned the first day of August.

September.

C. Itm. Henerie Robinson christened the xxj^th day.
C. Itm. Will'm Hamond christened the xxvij day.
C. Itm. John Jenkinson xpned the xvij^th day of October.
                                    November vac.

December.

B. Itm. Elizabeth Killingbeck buried the iiij day.
C. Itm. John Baker christened the xxj^th day.
B. Itm. John Baker buried the xxviij^th day.
                                    Januarius vac.

Februarie.

C. Itm. Jenet Stainton xpned the ix^th day.
C. Itm. John Huscroft christened the xxiij^th day.
C. Itm. ffraunc Brown xped the xvij day of March.

April, 1542.

C. Itm. An Weldayle xped the vj^th day.
C. Itm. Alice Hamond xped the x day.
C. Itm. Henry Young xped the iij day May.

June.

C. Itm. Margaret Ward xped the iiij day.
C. Itm. Will'm Tompson xped the xvj day.

Julie.

B. Itm. Jenet Cros buried the xxij^th day.
B. Itm. Jenet Browne buried the xxvj day.

August.

B. Itm. An Homes buried the xij^th day.
B. Itm. John Naute buried the xx^th day.

September.

B.   Itm. Agnes Nut buried the iij day.
C.   Itm. Robert Nut her son xped the same day.
C.   Itm. Arthure Hamond xped the xth day.
B.   Itm. John Nut & Will'm Allynson buried the xij day.
B.   Itm. Isabell Stokell buried the xiiij day.
C.   Itm. Agnes ffuster xped the xv day.

October.

M.   Itm. John Harbon & Jen^t Beregh married the vij day.

November.

B   Itm. Lawrence Lawson buried the xxxth day.
     Itm. December vacat.   Januarius vacat.

Februarie.

M.   Itm. John Smith & Jen^t Wright married the iij day.
C.   Itm. Alice Shippen xped the xvij day.
B.   Itm. the said Alice buried the xxiij day.
B.   Itm. Will'm Watkin buried the xxvj day.
C.   Itm. Jen^t Hay xped the xxviij day.
                              April vacat.

March, 1544.

C.   Itm. Thomas Smith xped the vjth daye.
B.   Itm. Thomas Shippen buried the xxviij day.

May.

C.   Itm. Jene^t Stainton xped the ij day.
B.   Itm. Will'm Johnson buried the iij day.
B.   Itm. Jen^t Baker buried xvth day.

June.

C.   Itm. Elsabeth Gyliam xped the xij day.
B.   Itm. John Ward buried the xxvijth day.

Julie.

C.   Itm. Thomas Pearson xped the xxiijth day.
B.   Itm. Jen^t Hav buried the xxvjth day.
B.   Itm. Alice Wells buried the xijth day of August.

September.

C.   Itm. John Hamond xped the vth day.
C.   Itm. John Bellobee xped the xxth day.
B.   Itm. Elsabeth Browne buried the xxj day.
C.   Itm. Agnes Dice xped the xxiij day.
B.   Itm. Joh. Olred buried the xxix day.

October.

M.   Itm. Wm Simson & Dorite Adam married the xix daye.
M.   Itm. Rob'rt Potter & Jen^t Cowper married the xxvj daye.

November.

B.   Itm. Isabell Roundell buried the ij day.
M.   Itm. Peter Docley and Jen^t Turpin married the xjth day.
M.   Itm. John Mewse and Elsabeth Ward married the xvjth day.

M. Itm. Thomas Dawson & Margaret Hallale married the xxiij day.
B. Itm. Jenet Robinson buried the xxiiij day.
M. Itm. Wm Butler & Cicele Adam married the xx° day.
C. Itm. Jen^t Smith xped the xvj day.
B. Itm. Agnes Dice buried the xxix day.

December.

C. Itm. ffraunc Mettham xped the iiij^th day.
B. Itm. Wm Hay buried the vj^th day.
C. Itm. ffraunc Younge xped the xi day.

Januarie.

C. Itm. Will'm Nawte xped the xj^th day.
B. Itm. John Bellobee buried the xiiij day.
B. Itm. Wm Tompson buried the xix day.
C. Itm. Peter Nelson xped the xxviij day.
B. Itm. Agnes Wilson vidua buried the vj of Februarie.
C. Itm. Wm Wheldale xped the vij day of March.

April vacat

May, 1545.

C. Itm. Alice Stokall xped the xviij^th day.
C. Itm. John Baker xped the xix day.
B. Itm. John Baker buried the xx^th day.
C. Itm. Rob'rt Nelson xped the xxj day.
C. Itm. Margaret Shippen xped the xxiiij day.
B. Itm. John Shippyn buried the same day.
B. Itm. Wm Robinson buried the xxvj day.
B. Itm. Margaret Shippen buried the xxix day.

June.

B. Itm. John Turpin buried the vj^th day.
B. Itm. Isabell Wise buried the xv^th day.

Julie.

M. Itm. Wm Bew and Jenet Byrton married the vth day.
B. Itm. Peter Nelson buried the xij day.
M. Itm. John Cros and Alice Staffurth married the xxj day.

August.

C. Itm. Henry Potter xped the iij day.
B. Itm. Thomas Smith buried the vij day.
B. Itm. Jen^t Whitley buried the xiij day.
B. Itm. Isabell Wheldayle buried the xv day.
C. Itm. Jen^t Simson xped the xv day.
B. Itm. Isabell Rawling buried the xxv^th day.
B. Itm. Thomas Pearson buried the xxvij^th day.

September.

C. Itm. Agnes Watt xped the first day.
B. Itm. Agnes Watkin buried the iiij^th day.
B. Itm. Rob'rt Wheldail buried the xth day.
B. Itm. Sr Peter Marciall buried the xxj day.

October.

B. Itm. Rob'rt Nelson buried the xth day.
B Itm. John Walker buried the xxvj day.
B. Itm. John Browne buried the xxix^th day.

November.

Itm. Isabell Bispam xped the v day.
Itm. John Tompson xped the xvth day.
. Itm. John Scrivener & Katteren Watkinson married the xvii day.
. Itm. Thomas Harrison & Mary Barmbow married ye xx day.

December.

Itm. Agnes Doncaster & Rob'rt Ward buried the iiij day.
Itm. Jen^t Dawson xped the xvjth day.

Januarie.

Itm. Jenet Dawson buried the first day.
Itm. Thomas Mewce xped the ij^o day.
. Itm. Katteren Bradford xped the xth day.
. Itm. Thomas Alan & Elizabeth Marshall married xvii die.
Itm. Rob'rt Barmbow buried the xviijth day.
Itm. Will'm Hemmingway buried the xxiijth day.
Itm. Will'm Richardson christened the xxiiijth day.

Februarie.

. Itm. John Birdsall & Alison Nelson married the xvj day.
Itm. Jen^t Marshall buried the xxjth day.
Itm. Isabell Townend buried the xxiijth day.
Itm. Will'm Wheldayl buried the xxiiij day.
Itm. Isabell Person xped the xijth day of March.

Aprill, 1546.

. Itm. John Dayle xped the xxijth day.
. Itm. M'gret Young xped the xxiijth day.

May.

. Itm. Agnes Hamond xped the ij day.
. Itm. Jenet Browne xped the vth day.

Junius vacat.

Julie.

. Itm. Margaret Butler xped the xvijth day.
. Itm. John Whitley & Isabell Hamond married the xviij day.
. Itm. John Hay xped the iij day of August.

September.

. Itm. Rob'rt Stones buried the xxijth day.
. Itm. Isabell Watt buried the xxv day.
. Itm. Joan Nelson xped the xxviijth day.
. Itm. Richard Marshall Dority Dockley married the xxixth day.

October vac.

November.

. Itm. Jan^t Dice xped the vth day.
. Itm. Rob'rt Awmond & Joan Prince married the vij day.
. Itm. John Awmond & An Watkin married the xiiij daye.
. Itm. Henry Turpin Isabel Hemingway married . . . .
. Itm. M'gret Shepherd xped the viijth day of December.

Januarie.

Itm. John Dawson buried the xxjth day.
. Itm. Xpofer Watt buried the xxijth day.

Februarie.

M. Itm. Rob'rt Boouth & Joan Barton married the first day.
B. Joan Berredge buried the second day.
B. Itm. Wheldail buried the xijth day.
C. Itm. Joan Marshall xped the xxvth day.
B. Itm. John Burton buried the xxvjth day.
C. Itm. Henry Huscroft xped the xxvij day.
B. Itm. ffraunces Smith xped the xx day of March.
B. Itm. Wm Watter buried ultimo die Martii, 1547.

Aprill, 1547.

C. Itm. M'gret Awmond xped the first day.
R. Itm. John Robinson buried the vijth day.
C. Itm. Thomas ffuster & Antony ffuster xped the xvth day.
B. Itm. Thomas ffuster buried the xxth day.
B. Itm. Elsabeth Wise buried the xxxth day.

May.

B. Itm. Anthony ffuster buried the xijth day.
C. Itm. Katteren Scrivener xped the xix day.
C. Itm. ffraunces Gilliam xped the xxij day.

June.

C. Itm. Katteren Whitley xped the third day.

July.

C. Itm. Will'm Shippen xped the third day.
C. Itm. Raulph Mettam xped the xxixth day.
C. Itm. John Awmond xped xxij° die August.

September.

C. Itm. John Baker xped the vth day.
B. Itm. Peter Cotes buried the vijth day.
C. Itm. Isabell Berredge xped the xxvijth day.

October.

M. Itm. John Longwood & Jane Hallalee married the second day.
C. Itm. Will'm Awmond xped the vijth day.
B. Itm. Jenet Berredge buried the xiijth day.

November.

B. Itm. Ralph Bispam buried the first day.
C. Itm. Katteren Awmond xped the same day.
M. Itm. Thomas Hamshire & M'gret Wheldayl married vj day.
M. Richard Hartley & Cicely Lawson married the xiij day.
M. Itm. Rob'rt Smith & M'gret Watt married the xxjth day.
B. Itm. John Dawson buried xxij° die Decembris.

Januarie.

C. Itm. ffraunces Nawte xped the second day.
C. Itm. Will'm Simson xped the vjth day.
B. Itm. Ralph Mettam buried the xxth day.
M. Itm. John Watkin & Jenet Browne married the xxiiijth day.

Februarius vacat.

Marche, 1548.

. Itm. An Belhowse xped the xxvjth day.
. Itm. Jen^t Mewse xped the xxixth day.

Aprilis vacat.

May.

. Itm. John Cowper & Will'm Person (Pearson) xped the first day.
. Itm. Alice Tompson xped the xth day.

June.

[. Itm. Lance Witley & M'gret hemingway married xvij° die.
. Itm. ffraunces Young xped the xxth day.

Julie.

. Itm. James Butler xped the xjth day.
. Itm. John Hamshire xped the xxixth day.

Augustus vac.

September.

. Itm. Jen^t Turpin xped the iiijth day.
. Itm. Janet Smith xped the vth day.
. Itm. Henry Longwood xped the xijth day.

October.

[. Itm. George Cutler & Alison Bispam married xiiij° die.
. Itm. Alison ffuster xped the xxijth day.
. Itm. Margaret Mitton xped the xxvth day.
. Itm. Edmund Cowper buried the xxvijth day.

November.

. Itm. Isabell Watkyn buried the viijth day.
. Itm. John Robinson xped the xiij day.
. Itm. Rob'rt Potter xped the xxij day.

December.

. Itm. Jen^t Richardson xped the vijth day.
. Itm. Will'm dawson xped the xvij day.
. Itm. John Shypherd xped xxx° die Januarii.
. Itm. An Nelson xped iiij° die ffebruarii.

March.

. Itm. Isabel Marshall buried the xth day.
. Itm. Margaret Mettam xped the xvth day.
. Itm. Alleson Tomson buried the xxjth day.

Aprill, 1549.

. Itm. Will'm Hamond xped the xiiijth day.

May.

. Itm. Ralph Hamond xped the vjth day.
. Itm. James Shippen xped the vjth day.
[. Itm. Thomas Taylor & Isabell Smith married the xiiijth day.

June.

. Itm. Mawd Carnaby & Agnes Mitton buried third day.
. Itm. Jen^t Wells buried the fift day.
[. Itm. Thomas Watkin & Isabell hemingway married the xxiijth day.

2

Julie.

M. Itm. Will'm hemingway & Agnes Barmbow }
Thomas Will'mson & Jenet Roundell married } the ixth day.
August vac.
C. Itm. Will'm Smith xped the ixth day of September.

October.

M. Itm. James Hall & Elizabeth Burton married the vjth day.
C. Itm. Jen^t Whitley xped the ixth day.
C. Itm. ffraunces Cowper xped the xiijth day.
B. Itm. Isabell Cowper buried the xxiijth day.

November.

B. Itm. Alleson Robinson buried the iij day.
C. Itm. Elizabeth Scrivener xped the vth day.
C. Itm. Richard Marshall & Jenet hamond xped the xvij day.
B. Itm. Jenet Nelson buried the xxth day.

December.

C. Itm. Katteren Behowse xped the ij day.
C. Itm. Isabell Tomson xped the viij day.

Januarie.

B. Itm. Cecile Hartley buried the viijth day.
C. Itm. John Gilliam xped the xth day.
C. Itm. Will'm Hemingway xped the xijth day.
B. Itm. John Gilliam buried the xxviijth day.

Februarie.

C. Itm. Thomas Smith xped the xth day.
C. Itm. Antonie Hawmeshire xped the xijth day.
B. Itm. Isabell Wilson buried the iij day of March.
C. Itm. M'gret huscroft xped the xxvijth day of March, 1550.

Aprill, 1550.

B. Itm. Thomas dongkaster buried the xxiijth day.
C. Itm. John Witley xped the xxiiijth day.
B. Itm. Will'm Burton buried the xxvth day.
M. Itm. Michaell ffuster & Elsabeth Woodhouse married xxix.
C. Itm. Thomas Watkin xped the vij day of May.
C. Itm. Alice Simson xped the xvth day of June.
C. Itm. Joan Mewse xped the xxvth day of June.
Julius vac.

August.

B. Itm. Saunder Marshall buried the xxth day.
B. Itm. Clemet . . . . . buried the xxjth day.
C. Itm. Isabel Mitton xped the ij day of September.

October.

C. Itm. Ames Longwood xped the xxjth day.
C. Itm. Richard Cotes xped the xxixth day.

November.

C. Itm. John Barker xped the vijth day.
C. Itm. Margaret Daweson xped the xxvjth day.
C. Itm. Alison Person xped the xxviijth day.

December.

I. Itm. Edward Richardson & Isabell person married the ij day.
. Itm. John Hamond xped the xxvjth day.

Januarie.

. Itm. John Crosse buried the vth day.
. Itm. Isabell Dockley buried the xxth day.

Februarie.

. Itm. Margaret Gilliam xped the xiiijth day.
. Itm. Margaret Robinson xped the xviijth day.

March.

. Itm. Edward Hamond xped the vjth day.
. Itm. Isabell Shepperd xped the xxth day.

Aprill, 1551.

. Itm. John Nawte xped the xxvth day.

Maius et Junius vac.

Julie.

. Itm. Thomas Wiseman xped the xviijth day.
I. Itm. John Dawson & Alice Richardson married the xxviij day.

August.

. Itm. An Shippen buried the xth day.
. Itm. John Nawte buried the xxjth day.
. Itm. Marrion Tutill & Alis Person buried the xxiiijth day.

September.

. Itm. John Shippen buried the iij day.
I. Itm. John Noble & Anes Emson married the vj day.
. Itm. Jen^t Dockley buried the xiiijth day.
. Itm. Ralf hamond buried the xxth day.
. Itm. Jen^t Potter xped the xxvth day.

October.

. Itm. Ralph Browne buried the vth day.
. Itm. Will'm Dockley buried the xixth day.

November.

. Itm. Anthony Turpin xped the ij day.
. Itm. Isabell Burton buried the xxth day.
. Itm. John Tomson buried the xxvjth day.

December.

. Itm. Rob'rt Boouth buried the xxjth day.
. Itm. Jan^t Boouth buried the xxiijth day.
. Itm. Johan Richardson xped the xxiij day.
. Itm. Thomas Whitley xped the xxiiijth day.
. Itm. Margaret Hamond xped the xxxjth day.

Januarie.

. Itm. dority Wiseman buried the iij day.
. Itm. Annes Ledum buried the iiijth day.
. Itm. An Watkin xped the vjth day.
. Itm. An Hemingway xped the xjth day.

February.

C. Itm. Richard Tomson xped the xj^th day.
C. Itm. An Hamond xped the xiiij^th day.
B. Itm. Richard Tomson buried the xxvij^th day.
C. Itm. Ralph Ledsam xped the ij^nd day of Marche.

         Aprilis vacat.

May, 1552.

C. Itm. Richard Hamshire xped the ij^nd day.

         June vac.

Julie

M. Itm. James Marshall & Margaret Adam married the vth day.
B. Itm. Johan Hemingway buried the vj^th day.
C. Itm. Will'm Whitley xped the xxix^th day.

August.

B. Itm. Will'm Whitley buried the vj^th day.
B. Itm. ffrauncs Huscroft buried the xxj^th day.

September.

B. Itm. Isabell Jenkinson buried the xvij day.
M. Itm. henry Medley & Isabel Nawlson married the xvij day.

October.

C. Itm. Will'm Mitton xped the iiij^th day.
C. Itm. John Nawte xped the viij^th day.
M. Itm. Thomas Humlock & Annes Merbeck married the xvj day.
M. Itm. Will'm Turpin & Elsabeth Ledum } married the xxiij^th day.
M. Itm. Antony Richardson & Alice Crud }

November.

C. Itm. John Smith xped the xx^th day.
C. Itm. An Smith xped the xxvij^th day.

December.

B. Itm. Margaret Awmond buried the xth day.
C. Itm. Agnes Marshall xped the xviij day.

         Januarius vac.

Februarie.

C. Itm. John Simson xped the vj^th day.
M. Itm. Will'm Tutill & Agnes Batman married the vij^th day.
B. Itm. ffrauncs Gilliam buried the ix^th day.

March.

B. Itm. John Robinson buried the ij day.
C. Itm. Johan Simson xped the vth day.

Aprill, 1553.

C. Itm. Janet Robinson xped the ij day.
B. Itm. Alison Marshall buried the xiiij^th day.
C. Itm. Jenet Wray xped the xvj^th day.

         Maius vac.

June.

 Will'm Wilson & Alis Person xped the first day.

I. Itm. Richard ffenteman & Joan ffynna married the iiijth day.
.. Itm. Katteren Cook & Annes Wray xped the xvj day of Julie.
    Now lacketh twoe yeres viz 1554 & 1555 and also as much as from this xvj day of Julie here next above written unto the iiijth day of December as followeth.

December, 1556.

I. Itm. Elsabeth Wilson buried the iiijth day.
I. Itm. John Smith buried the xvth day.
I. Itm. John Hembrowgh buried the xviijth day.
I. Itm. Katteren Coles buried the xxiiijth daye.

Januarie.

.. Itm. John Gisburn xped the iiijth day.
I. Itm. John Sykes buried the xxth day.
I. Itm. Jan^t hartley buried the xxvj day of februarie.

March.

I. Itm. Thomas Humlock buried the ij day.
.. Itm. An Marshall xped the iij^d day.
I. Itm. An ffenteman buried the xxxth day 1557.
I. Agnes Wells buried the xxijth day of Aprill 1557.

May, 1557.

I. Itm. An Young buried the xxj day.
I. Itm. Elinore Hallaly & Isabell Watter buried the xxij day.
I. Itm. John Dice & Jenet Shippen married the xxvjth day.
I. Itm. Sr John Gilliam buried the xxviij day.
I. Itm. William Caverley buried the ij day of June.

Julie.

I. Itm. Will'm Turpin & Agnes Humlock married the iiijth day.
.. Itm. Rob'rt Shypperd xped the xxixth day.

August.

I. Itm. Jenet Hembrough buried the iiijth day.
I. Itm. Agnes ffenteman buried the ixth day.
I. Itm. Will'm Hamond buried the xjth day.
I. Itm. Alison Scott buried the xviijth day.
    here lacketh one year viz.: 1558 and as much as from this day next above written unto the eight of October as followeth.

October 1559. *anno primo Regine Elizabethe.*

I. Itm. Will'm Taylor Jenent Smith married the viijth day.
I. Itm. Thomas Howdell of ffrieston buried the xxjth day.
I. Itm. William Gilliam of Hillom buried the xxiijth day.

November.

I. Itm. Robert Barden & Isabell Roundell married the vijth day.
I. Itm. Richard Hay of ffrieston buried the xth day.
I. Itm. Richard Wheldayl & John Netherwood married xix^o die.
.. Itm. Annes doughter of Ralf Roundell xped the xxiiijth day.
I. Itm. Elizabeth Biwater buried the xxiiijth day.
I. Itm. Wm Biwater & Joan Raling married the xxvjth day.
I. Itm. Richard Laycock and Joan Rimmington married the third day of December.
.. Itm. Thomas the son of Will'm Hinglebee of Shereburn xped the xvjth day of December.

B. Itm. Annes Doughter of Ralf Roundell buried xix^no die Decembris.
C. Itm. Alice Doughter of Thomas Shipperd xped the xiij^th day of Januarie.
M. Itm. Rob'rt thornton & Agnes Turpin married the xv^th Januarie.
M. Itm. Robert Marshall & Margaret gilliam married the xxj^th Januarii.
C. Itm. Barbara Hamond daughter of John hamond of hillom xped the xvj ffebruarii.
C. Itm. An the daughter of hugh Person of ffrieston xped the xviij^th day ffebruarii.
C. Itm. Will'm the son of John hallale of Milford was xped the xxix^th ffebruarii.
B. Itm. An the wief of hugh Person was buried the iij^o day Martii.
B. Itm. ffraunces son of John Browne buried the ix^th day of March

Anno d'ni 1560 et Elizabethe Reg'ne n'ri secundo.

B. Itm. Rob'rt the son of Thomas Shipperd of Burton buried the xxxj^o day of March.
B. Itm. Will'm son of Thomas Howdell of ffrieston buried the same day.
C. Itm. ffraunces doughter of Richard Wheldayl xped the same day.
B. Itm. Jen't a Bastard of Dority Marshall buried primo die Aprilis.
C. Itm. Margaret Doughter of John Nawte xped iij^o die Aprilis.
C. Itm. Rob'rt son of John Gisburn of Burton xped x^o die Aprilis.
B. Itm. Agnes Roundell of Monck frieston buried the same day.
C. Itm. John son of Anthony Richardson xped & buried xj^o Aprilis.
B. Itm. Rob'rt Gisburn buried the xxj^o day of Aprill.
B. Itm. Joan wief of Richard Wheldayll of Monckfrieston buried the xxij^o day of Aprill.
C. Itm. Simon Alleyn son of Thomas Alleyn of Shereburn xped xxvj^o die Aprilis.
C. Itm. Robert son of Will'm Dockley of hillom xped xxix^o die Marii.
M. Itm. Richard Lake & Joan Potter married xj^o die Junii.
M. Itm. Rob'rt Ward & Agnes Hey married xvj^o die Junii.
B. Itm. Agnes Turpin widow buried xxv^o die Junii.
M. Itm. Edward Dice & Alice Dawson married xxx^o Junii.
C. Itm. Katteren Ellis daughter of Edward Ellis of Monkfrieston xped ij^o die Julii.
M. Itm. Robert Nelson & Constance Woodhowse married vij^o Julii.
C. Itm. Agnes Pachet bastard to John Pachet of lodingde xped x^o die Julii.
C. Itm. An Yoyle daughter of Rob'rt Yoyle of Milforth xped xv^o die Julii.
C. Itm. Agnes Stansfeild daughter of Richard Stansfeild of Burton xped xix^o die Julii.
C. Itm. Joan Marshall daughter of John Marshall of Monkfrieston xped v^o die August.
C. Itm. Joan Mitton daughter of Wm Mitton of Burton xped xvij^o die Augusti.
M. Itm. Thomas Emson & Joan Halliday married xviij^o die Aug.
C. Itm. Will'm son of Wm Berredge of frieston xped xx^o die Augusti.
C. Itm. Joan daughter of Anthony Burton of hillome xped xix^o die Augusti.
C. Itm. Elsabeth daughter of Wm Burman of Milforth xped v^o die Septembris.
B. Itm. Agnes Patchet bastard of John Patchet of lodyngde was buried vij^o die Septembris.
B. Itm. Katteren Ellys daughter of Edward Ellys of Monkfrieston buried xvj^o die Septemb.
B. Itm. Alice Richardson wief of Peter Richardson of hillom buried xix^o die Septemb.
C. Itm. Agnes daughter of Wm Allely of Burton xped vij^o die Octobris.
C. Itm. John son of Wm Biwater of hillom xped xj^o die Octobris.
C. Itm. Xpian Crowder doughter of Robert Crowder of Burton xped the same day.
C. Itm. Dority daughter of Thomas Leaper of Shereburne xped xxix^o die Octobris.
C. Itm. Thomas son of John Dice of Milford xped iiij^o die Novembris.
M. Itm. Richard Wheldayle and An Turpyn Richard Turner & Isabell Nalson Richard Kirkby & Agnes Birkinshaw were married xxiiij^o die Novembris.
C. Itm. Agnes daughter of Peter Burton of Shereburn xped xiij^o die Decembris.

C. Itm. Rob'rt son of Richard Turner of Burton xped xiiijo die Decembris.
C. Itm. Alice doughter of Roger Sadler of Shereburn xped xvo die Januarii.
M. Itm. John Whitte & Agnes Sharpulls married xix Januarii.
C. Itm. John son of John Cotes of Monkfrieston xped xxvjo die Januarii.
C. Ellen daughter of Henry Nelstrop of Shereburn xped xxvijo die Januarii.
B. Itm. Elizabeth Taylor of Monkfrieston widow buried xxixo die Januarii.
C. Itm. Agnes daughter of Thomas Stedman of Shereburn xped xxxjo die Januarii.
C. B. Itm. Margaret daughter of Rob'rt Ward of Burton xped ijo die ffebruarii
and buried iijo die ejusdem.
B. Itm. John son of John Dockley of Monkfrieston buried xo die ffebruarii.
C. Itm. Joan doughter of George Burton of hillome xped viijo die ffebruarii.
B. Itm. W^m son of Peter Dockley of Monkfrieston buried xxiijo die ffebruarii.
B. C. Itm. Elsabeth doughter of John Nicolson of ffrieston buried ivo die Martii
the same day M'garet Nicolson her sister was xped.
B. Itm. Agnes late wief to Thomas Nelson of Monkfrieston buried ixo die Martii.
B. Itm. Margaret doughter of John Nicolson of Monkfrieston buried xiiijo die
Martii.

Anno d'ni 1561 : *et Regine Elizabethe* 3⁰.

C. Itm. John Dockley son of henry Dockley of hillome xped xxvo die Martii.
C. Itm. Joan Laycock doughter of Richard Laycock of Monkfrieston xped the
same day.
C. Itm. Peter Hemingway son of Will'm hemingway of hillome xped iijo die
Aprilis.
C. Itm. Joan Daughter of Ellen Laverock xped xxvijo die Martii & buried the same
day.
C. Itm. Margaret Barmbow daughter to James Barmbow xped xvjo die Aprilis.
B. Itm. Elizabeth Marshall of Monkfrieston buried ijo die Mensis Maii.
C. Itm. Agnes Crud daughter of Wm Crud of hillome xped vjo die Maii.
B. Itm. Jenet hartley of Burton married xvjo maii.
C. Itm. Elizabeth hartley daughter of Thomas hartly of Burton xped the same
day.
C. Itm. Elizabeth Scot daughter of Robert Scott xped xxjo die Maii.
C. Itm. Robert Spinck son of Thomas Spinck of hillome xped xxvijo die Maii.
C. Itm. Enssam Robinson doughter of John Robinson of Burton xped xxvijo die
Junii.
B. Itm. Agnes Robinson wief of Will'm Robinson of Burton buried ijo die Julii.
B. Itm. Anthony Bradforth was buried xiiijo die Julii.
C. Itm. M'garet daughter of Rob'rt Cowper xped vjo die Augusti.
C. Itm. Rob'rt son of thomas Emson xped xxijo die Augusti.
C. Itm. ffraunces daughter of Anthony Nelson xped xxviijo die Augusti.
B. Itm. Sr Xpofer Crumbock buried xxijo die Septembris.
B. Itm. Alice wief of Edward dice buried xxvo die Septembris.
B. Itm. Edward dice of Monkfrieston buried xxxo die Septembris.
B. Itm. Joan Doughter of John Longwood buried xxixo die Octobris.
B. Itm. Joan wief of Rob'rt Nelson buried xxxjo die Octobris.
B. Itm. Rob't Rawling of Monkfrieston buried ijo die Novembris.
B. Itm. Thomas Hartley and Agnes Marshall married ixo die Novembris.
B. Itm. Joan Doughter to John Nawte buried xiijo die Novembris.
B. Itm. John Nawte of Monkfrieston buried xiiijo die Novembris.
C. Itm. M'garet Doughter of Rob'rt Nelson xped viijo die Decembris.
C. Itm. John son of Richard Wheldayl xped vjo die Januarii.
C. Itm. John son of Edward Ellis xped vijo die Januarii.
M. Itm. Richard Turpin & Dority Netherwood married xiij Januarii.
M. Itm. Rob'rt Benet & Jane Ward married xxo die Januarii.
B. Itm. John Ward buried xxjo die Januarii.
B. Itm. Constance wief of Rob'rt Nelson buried xvo die decembris. this should
have been registered next to Margret Nelson 8 lines above.

M. Itm. Rob't Bennet & Joan Ward married xxº die Januarii.
C. Itm. Agnes Doughter of Ralf Roundayl xped xixº die ffebruarii.
B. Itm. Agnes Doughter of Ralf Roundayl buried xviijº die Martii.

Anno d'ni 1562 et Regine Eliz: 4º.

B. Itm. Ralf Growme of hillome buried vjº die Aprilis.
C. Itm. Elizabeth Doughter of henry Turpin xped xjº die Aprilis.
B. Itm. Jenet Benet of hillome buried viijº die Julii.
C. Itm. Katteren Doughter of Edward Richardson xped xº die Julii.
C. Itm. Joan Doughter of Will'm Mitton xped xvjº die Julii.
C. Itm. Elizabeth Doughter of Wᵐ Dockley xped xiiijº die Julii.
C. Itm. Roger son of Wᵐ Nelson of ffrieston xped ixº die Julii.
C. Itm. ffraunces Daughter of John Nicolson xped xxijº die Julii.
C. Itm. John Mason son of John Mason of hillom xped viijº die Augusti.
M. Itm. Galfridus Woodhowse & Margaret Hemswoorth married ixº die Augusti.
M. Itm. Hugh Person & Alice Ward married the same ixᵗʰ day.
M. Itm. Richard Owtwhayt & Elizabeth Rawling married xxº die Septembris.
C. Itm. Anthony son of Thomas Watkin of Hillom xped xxº die Septembris.
C. Itm. John son of John Dice of ffrieston xped xxiijº die Septembris.
C. Itm. Elizabeth Doughter of Richard Stansfield xped xxvijº die Septemb.
C. Itm. An Ward Doughter of Robert Ward of Burton xped primo die Octobris.
M. Itm. Henry Robinson of Burton and Alice Powle married iiijº die Octobris.
C. Itm. John Hallaley son of Wᵐ hallaley of Burton xped xxiijº die Octobris.
C. Itm. Margaret Turpin daughter of Richard Turpin of ffrieston xped xxviijº die Octobris.
B. Itm. Anthony Burton of hillom buried vjº die Novembris.
M. Item. John ffurth of the Parish of Shereburn & Alice Coyts of Monkfrieston married viijº die Novembris.
M. Itm. Thomas Barton of the Parish of Shereburn & Constance Maw of this parish married the viijº die Novembris.
M. Itm. Wᵐ White of the parish of Brayton & Agnes Carnabe of ffrieston married xvº die Novembris.
B. Itm. Thomas ffenteman of hillome buried xvijº die Novembris.
C. Itm. Margaret Laycock daughter of Ric Laycock of ffrieston xped primo die Decembris.
B. Itm. Katteren Person of ffrieston buried ixº die Decembris.
B. Itm. John Crowder Doughter of Ric Crowder of Burton buried xxixᵗʰ die Decembris.
B. Itm. Jenet Crowder wief of Ric Crowder buried xxixº die Decembris.
B. Itm. Wᵐ Mitton of Burton buried xxxº die Decembris.
B. Itm. Wᵐ Richardson of hillom buried iiijº die Januarii.
B. Itm. Jenᵗ Richardson of hillom widow buried vjº die Januarii.
B. Itm. Wᵐ Turner son of Ric Turner of Burton buried xvijº die Januarii.
M. Itm. Wᵐ Webster of the Parish of Swillington and Katteren Cowper married xvijº die Januarii.
C. Itm. Wᵐ Bywater son of Wᵐ Bywater of hillom xped xxjº die Januarii.
B. Itm. M'gret wief of Wᵐ Wells of hillom buried xxxº die Januarii.
M. Itm. John Mitton and Isabell Nawte married xxxjº die Januarii.
C. Itm. Jane Emson Doughter of Thomas Emson of Monkfrieston xped xxxjº die Januarii.
M. Itm. thom's Lund & Ellen Lilburn married vjº die ffebruarii.
C. Itm. ffraunces Wells son to John Wells of hillome xped xvº die ffebruarii.
C. Itm. Agnes Doughter of Jenᵗ Johnson xped xvjº die ffebruarii.
B. Itm. ffraunces Wells son to John Wells of hillom buried xxijº die ffebruarii.
C. Itm. Alice Spinck Doughter to Thomas Spinck of hillome xped xxiijº die ffebruarii.
C. Itm. Nicolas son of James Barmbow xped xijº die Martii.

Anno D'ni 1563 Regine Eliz: Quinto &c.

Itm. Roger son of Wm Nelson of frieston buried v^o die Aprilis.
Itm. James Mitton of Burton buried xxx^o die Maii.
Itm. Widow Bradford of hillome buried j^o die Junii.
Itm. Isabell Burton doughter of Anthony Burton of hillome xped xv^o die Junii.
Itm. Widow Johnson of ffrieston buried xxvij^o die Junii.
Itm. Ric Johnsons wief of frieston buried ij^o die Julii.
Itm. Jane filia populi xped the last day of Julie.
Itm. Robert Berridge son of Wm Berredge of Monk frieston xped iiij^o die Augusti.
Itm. Jane Roundayl doughter of Ralph Roundeyl xped xxix^o die Augusti.
Itm. John Person son of Hughe Pereson of ffrieston xped iij^o die Septembris.
Itm. Jane Roundayl doughter of Ralph Roundayl buried iij^o die Septembris.
Itm. James Baxter son of Will'm Baxter of Monk frieston xped xviij^o die Septembris.
Itm. Nicolas Hemmingway son of W^m hemmingway of hillome xped xxiiij^o die Septembris.
Itm. thoms Shepherd Wief of Burton buried xxj^o die Octobris.
Itm. Nicholas hallalie son of W^m hallale of Monkfrieston xped xv^o die Novembris.
Itm. Wm Bradford & Margaret Burton of hillome married xxiij^o die Novembris.
Itm. henry Robinson son of henry Robinson of Burton xped xxx^o die Novembris.
Itm. John Shippen son of John Shippen of hillome xped xxiiij^o die Decembris.
Itm. Isabell Burton Doughter of Anthony Burton of hillome buried xxix^o die Januarii.
Itm. thoms Richardson of frieston buried xix^o die Martii.

An'o D'ni 1564 Regine Eliz: n'ri Sexto.

Itm. Margaret Nelson Doughter of Anthony Nelson of Monkfrieston xped xxiij^o die Aprilis.
Itm. Will'm Richardson son of Edward Richardson of Hillome xped xxx^o die Aprilis.
Itm. Robert Hallalye son of Wm Hallalye of Burton xped xj^o die Maii.
Itm. Ralph Coyts son of John Coyts of Monkfrieston xped xj^o die Junii.
Itm. Elizabeth Hamond Doughter of John Hamond of hillome xped xviij^o die Junii.
Itm. Ralph Coytes son of John Coytes of Monkfrieston buried xxviij^o die Junii.
Itm. Wm Ward son of Rob'rt Ward of burton xped ix^o die Junii.
Itm. John Nelson son of Wm Nelson of Monkfrieston xped xxiij^o die Julii.
Itm. Thomas Bywater son of Wm Bywater of Hillome xped xxiij^o die Julii.
Itm. Agnes Hartley Daughter of Thomas Hartley of Burton xped xxx^o die Julii.
Itm. Elizabeth Bywater doughter of Thomas Bywater of Burton xped xiij^o die Augusti.
Itm. John Bradfurth son of John Bradfurth of Hillome xped j^o die Septembris.
Itm. Margaret Marshall daughter of John Marshall of Monkfrieston xped viij^o die Septembris.
Itm. John Smawlechar son of Edmund Smawlechar of Hillome xped primo die Octobris.
Itm. Isabell Laycock daughter of Richard laycock of Monkfrieston xped xviij^o die Octobris.
Itm. Robert Rayner and Anne Wells married v^o die Novembris.
Itm. Robert Cowper xped xij^o die Novembris.
Itm. Peter Bywater & Joan Nelson married xxvj^o die Novembris.
Itm. Robert Welles and Katteren Bradforth married ij^o die Novembris.
Itm. ffraunces Stansfeild doughter of Ric Stansfeild of Burton xped xvij^o die Decembris.

C. Itm. Isabell Turpin doughter of Henry Turpin of hillome xped xxiiijᵒ die decembris.
B. Itm. Isabell dice buried xxᵒ die decembris.
B. Itm. Arthure Pereson of hillome buried xxviijᵒ die Decembris.
C. Itm. Nicholas Ellys son of Edward Ellys of Monkfrieston xped vjᵒ die Januarii.
C. Itm. Margaret Roundayl Doughter of Ralph Roundayl of Monkfrieston xped xxviijᵒ die Januarii.
    Itm. Wᵐ son of Wᵐ Simson of hillome buried xijᵒ die Januarii.
C. Itm. Wᵐ Bradforth son of Wᵐ Bradforth of hillome xped xjᵒ die ffebruarii.
B. Itm. Richard Hamond of Hillome buried xiijᵒ die ffebruarii.
C. Itm. Isabell Wheldayll Doughter of Richard Wheldayll of Monkfrieston xped xxvjᵒ die ffebruarij.

Anno D'ni 1565 Regine Eliz: Septimo.

C. Itm. Joan Crowder doughter of Robert Crowder of Burton xped xxvᵒ die Martii.
M. Itm. Edward dunne and An Turpin married vjᵒ die Maii.
C. Itm. Mary Coytes daughter of John Coytes xped xxvijᵒ die Maii.
B. Itm. Edward Pereson of hillome buried eadem die p'dicto.
B. Itm. Joan Byrame doughter of John Byrome of hillome buried xxvijᵒ die Junii.
C. Itm. An Crudd doughter of Wᵐ Crudd of hillome xped xxixᵒ die Junii.
B. Itm. ffraunces Scotchburn doughter of Robert Scotchburn buried xxiiijᵒ die Julii.
M. Itm. Robert Nelson and Katteren Scrivener married xixᵒ die Augusti.
B. Itm. Will'm Nelson of Monkfrieston buried xvjᵒ die Septembris.
C. Itm. Enssame Robinson doughter of henry Robinson of Burton xped viijᵒ die Octobris.
C. Itm. Godfrey Rayner son of Robert Rayner of hillome xped xxiijᵒ die Septembris.
M. Itm. Richard Marshall and Jane Pearson married xiiijᵒ die Octobris.
B. Itm. Elizabeth Scrivener buried xviijᵒ die Novembris.
C. Itm. dorithie Shippen doughter of John Shippen of hillom xped xviijᵒ die Novembris.
M. Itm. Richard dolly and Alice Yoyle married xxvᵒ die Novembris.
B. Itm. Joan Dockley doughter of John dockly of Monkfrieston buried xxxᵒ die Novembris.
M. Itm. George Taylor and Margaret Baker married jᵒ die decembris.
B. Itm. John Scrivener of hillom buried vᵒ die decembris.
C. Itm. Will'm Wells son of Rob'rt Wells of hillome xped xxxjᵒ die decembris.
C. Itm. Wᵐ dockley son of henry dock'ey of hillome xped xxxjᵒ die decembris.
C. Itm. Nicholas Gilliam son of John Gilliam of hillome xped xiijᵒ die Januarii.
C. Itm. Richard Turner son of Richard Turner of Burton xped xiijᵒ die Januarii.
C. Itm. Katteren Barmbow doughter of James Barmbow of Monkfrieston xped xxᵒ die Januarii.
B. Itm. Eupham Robinson Doughter of henry Robinson of Burton buried xxiiijᵒ die Januarii.
B. Itm. John Robinson of Burton buried vᵒ die ffebruarii.
C. Itm. Katteren Nelson Doughter of Anthony Nelson of monkfrieston xped iiijᵒ die Martii.

Anno D'ni 1566 Regine Eliza: Octavo.

C. Itm. Joan Scot daughter of Robert Scot of Burton xped xxxᵒ die Martii.
B. Itm. Nicholas gilliam son of John gilliam of hillome buried iijᵒ die Aprilis.
C. Itm. Margaret Spinck doughter of thomas Spinck of hillome xped xxjᵒ die Aprilis.
C. Itm. Rob'rt gray son of Robert grey of Burton xped xxvᵒ die Aprilis.
B. Itm. An Shepherd doughter of thomas Shepperd of Burton buried xijᵒ die Maii.

C. Itm. M'garet houghton doughter of thomas howghton of Monkfrieston xped ix⁰ die Junii.
C. Itm. John Scrivener doughter of John Scrivener of hillome xped xvj⁰ die Junii.
B. Itm. Will'm Berridge son of Wᵐ Berridge of Monkfrieston buried xx⁰ die Junii.
C. Itm. Nicholas Dice son of John dice of Monkfrieston xped vij⁰ die Julii.
C. Itm. John Byrom son of John Byrom of hillom xped xxiiij⁰ Augusti.
C. Itm. John hallaley son of Wᵐ hallaley of Monkfrieston xped xxiiij⁰ die Augusti.
C. Itm. Edmund hallaley son of the said hallaley xped die predicto.
C. Itm. Edward hemmingway son of Will'm hemmingway of hillome xped j⁰ die Septembris.
B. Itm. Margaret Paddlethorp of hillom buried iij⁰ die Septembris.
C. Itm. Katteren Bywater doughter of Wᵐ Bywater of hillome xped xxj⁰ die Septembris.
C. Itm. Richard taylor son of george taylor of Monkfrieston xped xxvij⁰ die Octobris.
M. Itm. Peter Kirkby & An Spofforth married xvij⁰ die Novembris.
B. Itm. John hemmyngway son of Wᵐ hemmynway of hillome buried xj⁰ die Januarii.
C. Itm. hughe Spicer xped xij⁰ die Januarii.
C. Itm. Wᵐ Laycock son of Richard Laycock of Monkfrieston xped xix⁰ die Januarii.
M. Itm. John Gisburn & Jenet ffenteman married xix⁰ die Januarii.
M. Itm. Edward Wayneman & Margaret Hamshire married xxvj⁰ die Januarii.
C. Itm. Joan Turner doughter of Robert Turner of Burton xped ix⁰ die ffebruarii.
C. Itm. Margaret Watkin doughter of Thomas Watkin of hillome xped xvj⁰ die ffebruarii.
C. Itm. Richard Stansfeild son of Richard Stansfield of Burton xped xxiij⁰ die ffebruarii.
B. Itm. Richard Turpin of ffrieston buried xxvj⁰ die ffebruarii.
C. Itm. An Nelson doughter of Will'm Nelson of ffrieston xped xvj⁰ die Martii.

Anno D'ni 1567. *Regine Elisa : nono.*

B. Itm. Mary Biwater of burton buried xxvj⁰ die Martii.
B. Itm. Alison Cutler of hillome buried the same day.
B. Itm. John Sowersby of hillom buried iij⁰ die Aprilis.
B. Itm. John Whitley of hillom buried xiiij⁰ die Aprilis.
B. Itm. Isabell dockley of Monkfrieston & Joan her doughter buried xxij⁰ die Aprilis.
B. Itm. Rob'rt Skilbeck of Lumby buried viij⁰ die Maij.
M. Itm. dinys ffawshed and Joan Grayson married xv⁰ Junii.
B. Itm. Katteren doughter of Edward Richardson of Hillome buried xxiij⁰ die Junii.
C. Itm. Margaret Scotchburne doughter of Rob'rt Scotchburne of ffrieston xped xiij⁰ die Julii.
B. Itm. Richard Hasleleyby of hillom buried xiiij⁰ die Julii.
B. Itm. Jenet Benige a pore spiner in burton buried iij⁰ die Augusti.
B. Itm. Jane Hartley wief of John Hartley of hillome buried vij⁰ die Augusti.
B. Itm. Alice Nelson Sister to Will'm Nelson of ffrieston buried xiiij⁰ die Augusti.
C. Itm. John Gilliam son to John Gilliam of Hillome xped vij⁰ die Septembris.
B. Itm. Nicholas Barmbow buried ultimo die Septembris.
B. Itm. Will'm Turpin of hillom buried vij⁰ die octobris.
C. Itm. Edward Welles son of Rob'rt Welles of hillome xped ix⁰ die Novembris.
C. Itm. henry Marshall son of John Marshall of Burton xped die eodem ut supra.
B. Itm. John Welles of Hillome buried xj⁰ die Novembris.
C. Itm. Will'm Waud son of George Waud of ffrieston xped xvj⁰ die Novembris.
C. Itm. William Nelson son of Robert Nelson of ffrieston xped xiiij⁰ die Decembris.

C. Itm. Will'm Bradfurth son of John Bradfurth of Hillome xped xxviijo die
    decembris.
M. Itm. John Hartley of Hillome and Ellen Hasleyby married xxviijo die Januarii.
C. Itm. Will'm Spenser of Burton xped primo die ffebruarii.
B. Itm. ffraunces Richardson son of Edward Richardson of Hillome buried
    quinto die Martii.
C. Itm. Agnes Bradforth doughter of Will'm Bradforth of hillome xped vijo die
    Martii.
B. Itm. Agnes Hartley Doughter of thomas hartley of burton buried ixo die
    Martii.
B. Itm. Will'm dockley of hillom buried xviijo die Martii.

Anno d'ni 1568: *Regine Eliz: decimo.*

C. Itm. Thomas Roundeyl son of Ralph Roundeyl of ffrieston xped xxvo die
    Martii.
B. Itm. the sd. thomas Roundeyl buried xxviijo die Martii.
C. Itm. Katteren Rayner doughter of Rob'rt Rayner of hillome xped xviijo die
    Aprilis.
B. Itm. Will'm Crud of hillome buried xvo die Aprilis.
B. Itm. M'gret Smith of ffrieston buried xxvjo die Aprilis.
M. Itm. Rob'rt Underwood and Elizabeth Wells married ijo die Maii.
C. Itm. An Spinck doughter of thomas Spinck of hillome xped ixo die Maii.
C. Itm. Robert Hartley son of thomas hartley of Burton xped xxvijo die Maii.
B. Itm. Joan Gisburn doughter to John Gisburn of hillome buried vjo die Junii.
C. Itm. Nicholas Nelson son of Anthony Nelson of ffrieston xped xiijo die Junii.
C. Itm. Elizabeth Ellys doughter of Will'm Ellys of hillome xped xxo die Junii.
B. Itm. Richard Stansfield son of Richard Stansfield of Burton buried xxiijo die
    Junii.
C. Itm. Isabell doughter of Edward Ellys of ffrieston xped xxixo die Junii.
C. Itm. ffraunces daughter of Richard Laycock of ffrieston xped iiijo die Julii.
B. Itm. M'gret daughter Edward Richardson of hillome buried xjo die Augusti.
C. Itm. Thomas Crud son of Will'm Crud of hillome xped xxixo Augusti.
C. Itm. Alice dice daughter of John Dice of ffrieston xped xxvjo die Septembris.
B. Itm. Nicholas Nelson son of Anthony Nelson of ffrieston buried vo die
    Novembris.
B. Itm. Cicelie Butler buried xo die Novembris.
B. Itm. An Wilson of Hillome buried xo decembris.
C. Itm. Katteren Hartley doughter of John Hartley of hillome xped xijo die
    decembris.
C. Itm. david son of thomas diconson xped xixo decembris & buried xxvjo die
    ejusdem mensis.
C. B. Itm. david Howghton xped xxxo Januarii and buried primo ffebruarii.
C. Itm. Margaret Birom doughter to John Birom of hillome xped xiijo die
    ffebruarii.
C. Itm. Eupham Greene doughter to Richard greene of Burton xped xjo die Martii.

Anno d'ni : 1569 : *Reg : Eliz : undecimo.*

B. Itm. Margaret Richardson wief of John Richardson of Hillome buried xo die
    Aprilis.
C. Itm. Anthony wilton son of Rob'rt wilton of ffrieston xped xo die Aprilis.
C. Itm. Katteren Nettleton daughter of Will'm Nettleton of ffrieston xped xvijo
    die Aprilis.
C. Itm. John Barmbow son of James Barmbow of ffrieston xped jo Maii.
C. Itm. John Grave and ffraunces Grave children of Rob'rt Grave of Burton
    christened xixo die Maii.
B. Itm. Eupham Greene doughter of Richard greene of Burton buried xxiiijo die
    Maii.

C. Itm. Nicholas Stansfeild son of Richard Stansfield of Burton xped xij⁰ die Junii.
M. Itm. Thomas Langdayl & Jane Barmby married xxx⁰ Junii.
C. Itm. Edward Rayner son of Robert Rayner of Hillome xped xiiij⁰ die Augusti.
M. Itm. John Turpin and Elizabeth Rummans married xxj⁰ die Augusti.
M. Itm. Thomas diconson and Xpian Biwater married xviij⁰ Septembris.
B. Itm. Jane doughter of george Taylor of ffrieston buried eodem die ut ante.
C. Itm. Will'm son of Wilfride Hardwick xped xxj⁰ die Septembris.
B. Itm. Widow Welles of Hillome buried xxiij⁰ die Sept.
M. Itm. John Leaper and Jane Turpin married xvj⁰ Novemb.
C. Itm. Nicholas Wauld son of George Wauld of ffrieston xped vj⁰ die Novembris.
C. Itm. Henry Roundall son of Ralph Roundall of ffrieston xped xxv⁰ die decembris.
C. Itm. Agnes Emson doughter of thomas Emson of ffrieston xped primo die Januarii.
B. Itm. An Rayner wief of Robert Rayner of ffrieston buried xv⁰ ffebruarii.
    Itm. Julian Laycock doughter of Richard Laycock of ffrieston xped xvij⁰ die Martii.
C. Itm. Margaret Pereson doughter of Richard Pereson of hillome xped xix⁰ die Martii.
C. Itm. ffraunces Shippen doughter of John Shippen of Hillome xped xxij⁰ die Martii.

Anno d'ni 1570: Regine Eliz: 12.

Aprilis et maius vac.

C. Itm. Dorithie Loveday doughter of Robert Loveday of Burton xped xj⁰ die Junii.
C. Itm. Isabell Richardson doughter of Edward Richardson xped j⁰ die Octobris.
C. Itm. david Mettham son of Peter Mettham xped xiiij⁰ die Octobris.
C. Itm. Will'm ffletcher son of John ffletcher xped xxj⁰ die Octobris.
B. Itm. Julian Turpin wief of John Turpin buried xxiij⁰ die Octobris.
C. Itm. Robert Pereson son of Rob'rt Pereson of Burton xped xxv⁰ die Novembris.
C. Itm. ffraunces Howghton son of thomas howghton xped xxviij⁰ die decembris.
C. Itm. Agnes Gilliam doughter of John Gilliam of hillome xped j⁰ die Januarii.
B. Itm. Margaret wief of George Burton buried v⁰ Januarii.
B. Itm. Henry Turpin of hillom buried ix⁰ die Januarii.
B. Itm. Agnes wief of Willm ffletcher of ffrieston buried xij⁰ die Januarii.
C. Itm. doritie Green doughter of Richard Green of Burton xped xxviij⁰ die Januarii.

Anno d'ni 1571 : Regine Eliz. 13.

B. Itm. Margaret Nelson doughter of Rob'rt Nelson buried xiiij⁰ die Junii.
B. Itm. Katteren Leathom buried iiij⁰ Septembris.
M. Itm. ffraunces Bradley & Jenet Hunter married xiiij⁰ Augusti a⁰ p'dct.
M. Itm. John Pereson & Mary Spenser married xxix⁰ die Julii.
M. Itm. John Cotes and Isabell Nelson married xv⁰ die Octobris.
M. Itm. Thomas Heyfurth & dority Turpin married xviij⁰ die Octobris.
C. Itm. Richard Nelson son of Rob'rt Nelson xped xxv⁰ die decembris.
M. Itm. Will'm Webster & Isabell Turpin married xxiiij⁰ die Januarii.

Anno d'ni 1572 : Regine Eliz : 14.

C. Itm. Edward Shippen son of John Shippen xped viij⁰ die Aprilis.
C. Itm. Margaret Usler doughter of thomas Usler xped xxvij⁰ die Aprilis.
C. Itm. John ffox son of Will'm ffox xped iij⁰ die Maii.
C. Itm. Agnes Barmbow doughter of James Barmbow xped iiij⁰ die Maii.
C. Itm. Henry Mitton xped j⁰ die Junii.
C. Itm. Richard Marshall xped xv⁰ Junii.

C. Itm. John Robinson xped xiijº Julii.
C. Itm. Michael Pereson xped xxviijº Septembris.
C. Itm. John holmes p'ochie shereburn xped xijº Octobris.
C. Itm. thomas turpin p'ochie ejusdem xped xvjº Octobris.
C. Itm. Margaret dise & John Walker xped jº Novembris.
C. Itm. Thomas Spinck xped vijº die Novembris.
C. Itm. Margaret Pereson xped vijº die Novembris.
C. Itm. Katteren Scholey xped iijº die Januarii.
C. Itm. Will'm Roundall xped xxº ffebruarii.
C. Itm. John ffletcher xped vijº Martii.
C. Itm. ffraunces dice xped xjº die Martii.
B. Itm. Edmund Wells buried xº die Junii.
B. Itm. John Bowmer buried xxiijº die Julii.
B. Itm. George Taylor buried xxijº die Octobris.
B. Itm. Mary Pereson buried vjº die Novembris.
B. Itm. Jane dawson buried xiijº die Novembris.
B. Itm. William Hemmingway buried iijº die Januarii.
B. Itm. Edward Ellys buried vjº die Januarii.
B. Itm. Will'm Bradforthe buried xixº die ffebruarii.
B. Itm. dority green & Jenet Netleton buried xxijº ffebruarii.
B. Itm. Elizabeth Tyrpin buried vijº die Martii.

Anno d'ni 1573: Regine Eliz: 15.

B. Itm. Will'm Casson buried xxjº die Martii.
C. Itm. Jane diconson xped iiijº die Aprilis.
C. Itm. Will'm Cowper xped xjº die Aprilis.
M. Itm. John Morlayn & M'gret Metham married iijº die Maii.
B. Itm. Henry Young buried xvº die Maii.
C. Itm. Henry Hemingway buried xixº die Maii.
C. Itm. Thomas Nettelton xped xxvijº die Junii.
C. Itm. Robert Boulton xped xxvijº die Septembris.
M. Itm. John Pereson & Jenᵗ Meuse married iijº die Octobris.
C. Itm. thomas hartle a bastard xped xº die Octobris.
C. Itm. Margery Robinson xped xxvº Octobris.
C. Itm. Edward Grysedell xped xº die Novembris.
B. Itm. the sd. Edward buried xixº die decembris.
C. Itm. Jane Laycock xped xvjº die Januarii.
B. Itm. . . . . Shippen buried xxijº die Januarii.
C. Itm. Richard Gilliam xped xxº die ffebruarii.

March 1574 Regine Eliz 16.

B. Itm. Margaret Spencer buried the Last day.

Aprill.

C. Itm. Margaret Morleyn xped xjº die.

May.

C. Itm thomas Leaper xped xjº die.

Junius vac.
July.

B. Itm. An Wheldayl buried ultimo die.

August.

B. Itm. Elizabeth Bradley buried viijº die.

September.

C. Itm. Will'm Longwood xped xº die.
C. Itm. Margaret Muse xped eodem die.

October.

C. Rob'rt Halleley xped ij° die.

November.

B. Itm. Jenet Roundayl buried j° die.
B. Itm. Ralph Scrivener buried v° die.
B. Itm. Will'm Longwood buried viij° die.

December.

B. Itm. Anthony Nelson buried ix° die.

Januarie.

C. Itm. doritie Houghton xped j° die.
C. Itm. Richard Johnson xped xvj° die.
C. Itm. Margaret Walker xped xvj° die.
B. Itm. Jent Richardson buried xxiiij° die.
C. Itm. John Mitton xped xxx° die.

ffebruarie.

B. Itm. Will'm Mowberley buried v° die.
B. Itm. Roger Greene buried xix° die Martii.

March 1575. *Regine Eliz :* 17.

B. Itm. Rob'rt Bywater buried xxviij° die.

Aprilis vac.

May.

M. Itm. Rob'rt Lawson & Jane Meuse married xv° die.
C. Itm. Alice Stansfeild xped xxij° die.
M. Itm. Will'm Headley & Margery Rokesby married xvj° die.

June.

C. Itm. Margaret Pereson xped xij° die.
B. Itm. Margaret Marshall buried xxiij° die.

Julius et August vac.

September.

C. Itm. Isabell Hustler xped iij° die.
C. Itm. Margaret Hamond xped xiiij° die.
C. Itm. Rob'rt Campinet xped xxvj° die.

October.

B. Itm. Isabell Tomlinson buried vij° die.
M. Itm. Henry Boouth & Katteren Whitley married xxx° die.

November.

M. Itm. Rob'rt Knowles & Margaret Nicolson married xiij° die.
B. Itm. John Gisburn buried ultimo die.

December et Januarie vacant.

ffebruarie.

C. Itm. George Lawson xped iij° die.
C. Itm. Margaret Richardson xped xvij° die.
C. Itm. Will'm Baker xped xj° die Martii.
B. Itm. John Layton buried xij° die Martii.
C. Itm. Will'm diconson xped xix° die Martii.

March 1576 Regine Eliz. 18.

Martius et Aprilis vac.

May.

B. Itm. Will'm diconson buried xix⁰ die.
C. Itm. Elizabeth Longwood xped xx⁰ die.

June.

B. Itm. George Lawson buried xij⁰ die.
C. Itm. Margaret Calverd xped xxiij⁰ die.

Julie.

B. Itm. Agnes Metham buried ij⁰ die.
C. Itm. Rob'rt Bradley xped xij⁰ die.

August.

C. Itm. Richard Bolton xped v⁰ die.
B. Itm. Agnes Pereson buried xiiij⁰ die.
C. John Muse xped xxvj⁰ die.

September vac.

October.

B. Itm. Richard Tomlinson buried v⁰ die.
B. Itm. Rob'rt Marshall buried vj⁰ die.
B. Itm. Agnes Hamond buried xj⁰ die.
B. Itm. John Mayson buried xxvij⁰ die.

November.

C. Itm. Martyn Shippen xped xj⁰ die.
M. Itm. John Hueson & Agnes . . . . . maried xiij⁰ die.
C. Itm. John Johnson & Will'm Johnson xped xx⁰ die.

December vac.

Januarie.

C. Itm. Elizabeth Hollingworth xped j⁰ die.
B. Itm. Jenet Berredge buried xvij⁰ die.
C. Itm. Will'm Gilliam xped xxiij⁰ die Martii.
C. Itm. Joseph ffletcher xped xxiiij⁰ die Martii.

Aprill 1577 : Regine Eliz : 19.

B. Itm. Elizabeth Simson buried xij⁰ die.
B. Itm. Robert Bradley buried xvij⁰ die.
C. Itm. Will'm diconson xped xvij⁰ die.
C. Itm. Will'm dice xped xxij⁰ die Aprilis.

May.

B. Itm. John Pereson buried vj⁰ die.
C. Itm. Rob'rt Leaper xped viij⁰ die.
C. Itm. Richard Smith xped x⁰ die.
M. Itm. Hugh Coltris & Elizabeth Gray married xj⁰ die.
B. Itm. Will'm dockley buried xxv⁰ die.

June.

C. Itm. Will'm Wilson xped iiij⁰ die Junii.
B. Itm. Ux Hey buried xxx⁰ die.

Julie.

C. Itm. Wᵐ Nelson son of ffraunces Nelson xped xxijᵒ die.
M. Itm. Ric hutchinson & Agnes pereson maried xxxᵒ die.
August vac.

September.

C. Itm. Margret Bradley xped xvᵒ die.
C. Itm. Alice Lawson xped ead die.
B. Itm. Ellen Netleton buried xxᵒ die.

October.

C. Itm. Will'm dawson xped iijᵒ die.
C. Itm. Launcelot pereson xped vjᵒ die.
C. Itm. Isabell Walker xped xiijᵒ die.
M. Itm. John Atkin & Jenet dice maried xiijᵒ die.

November.

M. Itm. Will'm Pereson & An Whitley married xᵒ die.

December.

B. Itm. John Taylor buried iiijᵒ die.
B. Itm. Elizabeth Stansfeild buried xijᵒ die.

Januarie.

B. Itm. Elizabeth Gayton buried xᵒ die.
M. Itm. John Simson & Alice wilton married xixᵒ die.

Februarie.

C. Itm. James Hamond xped ijᵒ die.
B. Itm. ffraunces Stansfeild buried iiijᵒ die Martii.
B. Itm. thomas Watkin buried xixᵒ die Martii.

Aprill 1578 Regine Eliz 20.

M. Itm. thomas Loveday and Agnes Spofourth married xxᵒ die.
C. Itm. Will'm Mitton xped xxᵒ die.

May.

M. Itm. Ralph Roundell & Elizabeth Utting maried xxiijᵒ die.
C. Itm. Margaret Coltres doughter of hugh Coltres xped xiijᵒ die.
C. Itm. John Morleyn son of John Morlayn xped xxxᵒ die.

June.

C. Itm. Margaret Atkin doughter of John Atkin of Lumby xped ijᵒ die Junii.
C. Itm. James Hutchinson son of Richard hutchenison xped xxᵒ die.
C. Itm. Gervase dice son of John dice xped xxvijᵒ die.

Julie.

C. Itm. Mary doughter of david Calverd xped jᵒ die.
M. Itm. Thomas Graunge & An hemingway married vjᵒ die.
September vac.

October.

C. Itm. Will'm Pereson xped jᵒ die.
C. Itm. Katteren Tomson xped vᵒ die.
M. Itm. ffraunces Smith & Jenᵗ Naulson married xxiiijᵒ die.
C. Itm. Jenᵗ Meuse xped xxvjᵒ die.
B. Itm. Mary Cotes buried xxixᵒ die.

4

November.

M. Itm. George Wray & Jen^t Wilson maried vij^o die.
C. Itm. Will'm Bradley xped x^o die.
C. Itm. Margret Bradley xped xiij^o die.

December.

C. Itm. John Austinson xped v^o die.
C. Itm. Will'm Bew xped xxvij^o die.

Januarie.

B. Itm. Thomas Biwater buried vj^o die.
B. Itm. Alice Johnson wief of Oswould Johnson buried xxx^o die.
C. Itm. Thomas Gaton xped xxxj^o die.

Februarie.

C. Itm. Jen^t Longwood xped vj^o die.
B. Itm. Gervase dice buried vij^o die.
C. Itm. John Wray son of George Wray xped xj^o die.
B, Itm. An doughter of Ric. green of Burton buried xix^o die.
B. Itm. John Wraye son of george Wray buried xxj^o die.
C. Itm. Katteren Smith doughter of thomas Smith xped viij^o die Martii.
B. Itm. Robert Richardson a Servant at Nelson wieves of the hill buried xvj^o die Martii.

Aprill 1579. Regine Eliz : 21.

B. Itm. Agnes Bower buried j^o die.
B. Itm. Elizabethe Murgetrod buried xxiiij^o die.

May.

B. Itm. Margaret Marshall buried iij^o die.
B. Itm. John Morley son of John Morlay buried viij^o die.
C. Itm. Agnes Bolton xped x^o die.
C. Itm. Elizabethe Huscroft doughter of henry Huscroft of Burton xped xiij^o die.

June.

B. Itm. the sd. Elizabeth huscroft buried v^o die.

Julie.

B. Itm. Robert Nelson buried xix^o die.
C. Itm. dorithie Hollingworthe xped xix^o die.
M. Itm. John Jackson & Jenet Allayn maried xxv^o die.

August.

M. Itm. Anthony Brown & M'gret diconson maried viij^o die.
C. Itm. W^m halleley son of W^m hallely of frieston xped xix^o die.

September.

C. Itm. Mathew Nelson son of ffraunces Nelson xped viij^o die.

October.

B. Itm. dorithe hollingworthe buried vj^o die.
B. Itm. Margaret Stevenson wief of John Stevenson buried viij^o die.
B. Itm. Ellyn Baker widow buried xiiij^o die.
B. Itm. thomas Spinck son of thomas Spink buried xvj^o die.

November.

B. Itm. John Stevenson buried x^o die.
C. Itm. Isabell diconson doughter of thomas diconson of ffrieston xped xxiiij^o die.

December.

B. Itm. ffraunces Gilliam daughter of John Gilliam buried xvᵒ die.

Januarie.

B. Itm. An wefe of John Bradley buried xᵒ die.

C. Itm. Isabell & Elizabethe hamond children of Wᵐ hamond xped xxᵒ die.

Februarie.

B. Itm. Richard Cotes buried jᵒ die.

C. Itm. Will'm Turpin son of John Turpin of ffrieston xped vᵒ die.

B. Itm. John Wells son of Rob'rt Wells buried xijᵒ die.

C. Itm. Thomas Mayson son of Thomas Mayson xped xixᵒ die.

B. Itm. Will'm Johnson buried xxiijᵒ die.

March 1580. Regine Eliz : 22.

C. Itm. Mary Shippen doughter of James Shipen xped xxvjᵒ die.

Aprill.

C. Itm. John Colley xped xxxᵒ die.

May.

M. Itm. Ralph Roundell & Elizabeth Nelson maried iijᵒ die.

B. Itm. Agnes Turpin daughter of thomas Heyforthe wief buried iiijᵒ die.

M. Itm. John Bradley and Julian Nelson maried xvijᵒ die.

June.

C. Itm. John Muncaster a bastard xped xixᵒ die.

C. Itm. John Hutchinson son of Richard hutchinson xped xxvjᵒ die.

Julie.

C. Itm. John Walker son of thomas Walker of hillome xped iiijᵒ die.

C. Itm. John Wright daughter of thomas Wright of hillome xped xxiiijᵒ die.

C. Itm. Jenet Bolton doughter of thomas Bolton of Burton xped xxvᵒ die.

August.

B. Itm. Gervase Boouthe son of henry Boouthe of Birkin buried jᵒ die.

C. Itm. Isabell Pereson daughter of Will'm Pereson of hillom xped xjᵒ die.

C. Itm. ffraunces Wray doughter of george wray xped xxjᵒ die.

B. Itm. Isabell Pereson aforesaid buried xxvjᵒ die.

September.

C. Itm. John Tomson son of ffraunces tomson widow xped xjᵒ die.

B. Itm. Mary Calverd daughter of david Calverd buried xxᵒ die.

October.

C. Itm. . . . . . Will'm Calverd son of david Calverd xped ijᵒ die.

B. Itm. Elizabethe Beredge doughter of Will'm Beredge of hillome buried vjᵒ die.

C. Itm. Jenet Hollingwoorth doughter of Lyonell hollingwoorth of Burton xped xjᵒ die.

C. Itm. ffraunces Austinson doughter of thomas Austinson xped xvijᵒ die.

November.

C. Itm. Will'm Browne son of Anthony Browne xped xixᵒ die.

M. Itm. Richard Campinet & Jenet Ward maried xxiiijᵒ die.

M. Itm. James ffletcher and Elizabethe ffletcher maried xxvijᵒ die.

B. Itm. ffraunces Austinson doughter of thomas Austinson above named buried xxviijᵒ die.

December.

C. Itm. ffraunces Morlayn doughter of John Morlayn xped xiijº die.

C. Itm. Will'm Pereson & Ellyn Pereson children of Robert Pereson of Burton xped xxiiijº die.

C. Itm. ffraunces Roundell doughter of Ralphe Roundell xped xxviijº die.

Januarie.

M. Itm. Will'm Berredge & Alice Goodard maried xxjº die.

C. Itm. An Turpin a Bastard doughter to Katteren Turpin xped xxviijº die.

Februarie.

B. Itm. Isabell Bolton wief of John Bolton of Burton buried xixº die.

C. Itm. ffraunces Coltres son of Hugh Coltres xped xixº die.

C. Itm. Thomas Gilliam son of John Gilliam xped xxº die.

B. Itm. Constance Turpin widowe buried xxviijº die.

B. Itm. ffraunces Coltres above said buried viijº die Martii.

Aprill 1581. *Regine Eliz: 23.*

B. Itm. John Whitley buried jº die.

B. Itm. Abraham Boouth buried xvijº die.

May.

C. Itm. thomas Bew son of thomas Bew of hillome xped ijº die.

C. Itm. Jane Meuse doughter of thomas Muse xped iiijº die.

M. Itm. Edmund Playfear and ffraunces tomson maried xjº die.

Junius vac.

Julie.

B. Itm. Henry dockley buried vjº die.

B. Itm. Richard Halalie son of Will'm hallalie buried viijº die.

August.

M. Itm. Oswould Joneson and Margaret Bosse maried xxvijº die.

September.

M. Itm. Nicholaus Cowpland and Jenet Marshall married xxxº die.

October.

M. Itm. John Bolton and Agnes Stansfield maried viijº die.

B. Itm. Rob'rt Underwood buried ixº die.

November.

C. Itm. Elizabeth Campinet doughter of Richard Campinet xped xjº die.

C. Itm. Ellen Taylor doughter of one Brian Taylor a Londoner xped xjº die.

C. Itm. John Mitton son of henry Mitton xped xvº die.

M. Itm. Richard Hemmingway & An dockley maried xxvjº die.

C. Itm. Rob'rt Hamond son of Arthure Hamond xped xxxº die.

December.

M. Itm. Will'm Hemmingway of Hillome buried xxiijº die.

C. Itm. Margaret Berredge doughter of Will'm Berredge of Hillome xped xxxº die.

Januarie.

M. Itm. John Hawmond and Margaret Shepperd maried xvjº die.

C. Itm. Brian Austinson son of Thomas Austinson xped xxº die.

C. Itm. John Longwood son of Henry Longwood of Burton xped xxviijº.

Februarie.

C. Itm. Thomas Nelson son of ffraunces Nelson xped iij° die.

March.

C. Itm. dorithy Pereson daughter of Will'm Pereson of hillome xped viij° die.
C. Itm. Will'm Hamond son of John Hamond of hillome xped xj° die.

Aprill 1582. *Regine Elis :* 24.

C. Itm. Ralph Bradley son of ffraunces Bradley xped xxiij° die.
                    Maius vac.

June.

B. Itm. . . . . . Becket of Leeds buried ij° die.

Julie.

B. Itm. John Wharledayl a childe buried xxiiij° die.
C. Itm. Margaret Wells daughter of Rob'rt Wells of hillom xped xxv° die.
B. Itm. Margaret Marshall Widow buried xxviij° die.

August.

C. Itm. John Hemmingway son of Richard Hemmingway xped j° die.
C. Itm. ffraunces Hemmingway daughter of the sd. Ric. hemmingway xped j° die.

September.

B. Itm. John Hartley son of thomas Hartley buried xxviij° die.
C. Itm. Jane Browne daughter of Anthony Browne xped xxx° die.

October.

B. Itm. Will'm Hallaley son of Will'm hallale of ffrieston buried xvj° die.
B. Itm. An dockley doughter of John dockley buried xxviij° die inquam xxvj° die.
C. Itm. John Procter son of Edward Procter xped xxviij° die.

November.

C. Itm. Isabell Mason doughter of thomas Mason xped xiij° die.

December.

C. Itm. dorithie Roundell daughter of Ralph Roundell xped vj° die.
C. Itm. Elizabethe Bolton daughter of John Bolton xped xx° die.
C. Itm. dorithie Hallaley daughter of Will'm hallaley of ffriston xped xxvij° die.
B. Itm. dorithy Simpson widow buried xxxj° die.

Jannuarie.

B. Itm. thomas Hartley buried xiiij° die.
C. Itm. dorithy Hutchinson doughter of Richard Hutchinson xped xxj° die.
B. Itm. John Allen a Bastard buried xxij° die.
C. Itm. Margaret Baker daughter of John Baker xped xxiiij° die.
B. Itm. dorithye Hutchinson above said buried ultimo die.

Februarie.

B. Itm. dorithie Hallabie buried v° die.
B. Itm. Agnes Cotes of Beal widow buried x° die.
C. Itm. Christopher Wilson son of Mr Will'm Wilson xped xij° die.
B. Itm. John Halleley son of Will'm Hallaley buried xxviij° die.
B. Itm. John Davison buried xj° die Martii.

March 1583.   Regine Eliz : 25º.

B. Itm. Agnes Smith buried xxviijº die.
B. Itm. Margaret Wells doughter of Robert Wells buried xxixº die.

Aprill.

C. Itm. Elizabeth diconson xped xixº die.

May.

C. Itm. Margret Rawling a bastard xped jº die.

June.

C. Itm. ffraunces Shippen doughter of James Shippen xped ixº die.

Julie.

C. Itm. Elizabeth Skilbeck doughter of John Skilbeck xped vijº die.
B. Itm. Agnes Crud a mayd buried vijº die.
C. Thomas Shippen son of John Shippin xped xxjº die.

August.

C. Itm. George Turpin son of John Turpin xped xxxº die.

September.

C. Itm. Will'm Crowder son of George Crowder xped iiijº die.

October.

C. Itm. Elizabeth Coltres doughter of Hugh Coltres xped xxiijº die.

November.

C. Itm. John Morlay son of John Morlay xped xxixº die.

December.

C. Itm. Alice Bew doughter of thomas Bew xped at Birkin xxixº die.

Januarie.

M. Itm. Will'm Barmbee & Sibill Barden maried xiiijº die.
C. Itm. Agnes Hallaley doughter of Will'm Hallaley xped xxvjº die.
M. Itm. Mr Will'm Allen & Mrs Katteren Banister maried xxvijº die.

Februarie.

M. Itm. Edmund Thorneton & Elizabeth Stansfeild maried ijº die.
B. Itm. ffraunces Hemingway doughter of Richard Hemingway buried xxº die.
M. Itm. John Taylor & Alice Bolton maried xxvijº die.
C. Itm. Peter son of Ric. hemingway xped xxvijº die.

March.

B. Itm. George Burton buried vjº die.
C. Itm. Nicholas Muse xped xjº die.

April vac.

May 1584: Regine Eliz : 26.

C. Itm. Margaret Gilliam doughter of John Gilliam xped xjº die.
C. Itm. Margaret Wray doughter of George wray xped xiijº die.
C. Itm. Rob'rt Hamond son of John Hamond xped xxxº die.

June.

C. Itm. Joseph son of thomas Wright xped xijº die.
M. Itm. Nicolas dean & Margaret Redia . . . . maried xvjº die.

Julie.

Itm. Jane Bywater buried xiiij⁰ die.
Itm. Nicholas Briggs son of John Briggs xped xxj⁰ die.

August.

Itm. ffraunces Bolton doughter of thomas Bolton xped j⁰ die.
Itm. Richard Collet son of Will'm Collet xped ix⁰ die.
Itm. Stephen Nelson son of ffraunces Nelson xped xxvij⁰ die.

September.

Itm. Mary Baker doughter of John Baker xped viij⁰ die.
Itm. Agnes Lussall buried xv⁰ die.

October.

Itm. Thomas Smith buried viij⁰ die.
Itm. George Rawson son of John Rawson xped xxv⁰ die.

November.

Itm. John ffeildon and Isabell Rayner maried viij⁰ die.

December.

Itm. Millesans Thornton doughter of Edmund Thornton xped xxvij⁰ die.

Januarie.

Itm. Thomas Barmbee son of Will'm Barmbee xped viij⁰ die.
Itm. Rob'rt Mason son of Thomas Mason xped xij⁰ die.
Itm. Agnes Bolton wief of John Bolton buried ultimo die.

Februarie.

Itm. Millesans Thornton buried xiiij⁰ die.
Itm. Margaret Roundell buried xxviij⁰ die.

Martius vac.

Aprill 1585. *Regine Eliz :* 27.

Ralphe Bradley son of ffraunces Bradley buried viij⁰ die.
Itm. ffraunces Shippen doughter of John Shippen xped xxviij⁰ die.

May.

Itm. dorithy Stansfeild doughter of Richard Stansfeild buried ij⁰ die.
Itm. An Dockley buried xj⁰ die.

June.

Itm. Hughe Pereson buried xxij⁰ die.
Itm. Christopher Stones and Agnes Ward maried xxvij⁰ die.

Julie.

Itm. Isabell Mitton wief of John Mitton buried vij⁰ die.
Itm. Ellen Scrivener doughter of ffraunces Scrivener xped xvj⁰ die.
Itm. John Mitton buried xvij⁰ die.

August.

Itm. John dice buried vij⁰ die.
Itm. Batholomew Longwood son of Henry Longwood xped xxij⁰ die.

September.

Itm. ffraunces Nelson buried vj⁰ die.
Itm. Mary dean doughter of Nicholas dean xped vij⁰ die.

C.   Itm. Nicholas diconson son of thomas diconson xped xxvᵒ die.
C.   Itm. dorothie Bradley daughter of ffraunces Bradley xped xxixᵒ die.

October.

C.   Itm. Will'm Hemingway son of Richard hemingway xped vijᵒ die.
C.   Itm. Will'm Berridge son of Will'm Berridge of Hillome xped xiiijᵒ die.
B.   Itm. Alice Berridge wief of the sd. Will'm Berridge buried xxijᵒ die.
M.   Itm. Nicholas Procter Minister of this Parish and Jane Nelson maried xxvjᵒ
        die.
C.   Itm. John Skilbeck son of John Skilbecke xped xxxᵒ die.

November.

B.   Itm. Ralph Roundell buried vjᵒ die.
B.   Itm. Nicholas dean buried xvᵒ die.
C.   Itm. Nicholas Mitton son of Henry Mitton xped xvjᵒ die.
M.   Itm. Brian dawson and Agnes Loveday maried xxvijᵒ die.
M.   Itm. Will'm Wilie and dorithie Smithe maried xxviijᵒ die.
B.   Itm. Elizabeth Hallaley wief of Will'm Hallaley buried xxxᵒ die.

December.

M.   Itm. Alexander daniell and Agnes Marshall maried vᵒ die.
M.   Itm. Eliseus Lumas and Margaret Tenand maried xiiijᵒ die.
B.   Itm. dorothie Bradley daughter of ffraunces Bradley buried xvᵒ die.
B.   Itm. Will'm Atkinson buried xvjᵒ die.
C.   Itm. Ralph Roundell son of Elizabeth Roundell widow xped xviijᵒ die.
B.   Itm. Nicholas diconson son of Thomas diconson xped buried xxᵒ die.
B.   Itm. ffraunces Bradley wief called Jenet Bradley buried xxixᵒ die.

Januarie.

B.   Itm. John Simson buried jᵒ die.
B.   Itm. Elizabeth Hall buried vᵒ die.
B.   Itm. Nicholas Nowell buried xjᵒ die.
B.   Itm. Ric. Berridge buried xjᵒ die.
C.   Itm. Elizabeth hamond doughter of Jo: hamond xped xijᵒ die.
B.   Itm. ffraunces Bradley buried xvijᵒ die.
B.   Itm. John Richardson buried xixᵒ die.
C.   Itm. Elizabeth Colliet doughter of Richard Colliet xped xxviijᵒ die.
B.   Itm. Alice Crowder wief of George Crowder buried xxxᵒ die.

Februarie.

C.   Itm. John Thornton son of Edmund Thornton xped xiiijᵒ die.
B.   Itm. Elizabethe Nelson widow buried xxijᵒ die.
B.   Itm. John Thornton above said buried xxvᵒ die.

March.

C. B. Itm. Jane Shippen doughter of James Shippen xped jᵒ die & buried viijᵒ die.
B.   Itm. Rob'rt Crowder buried xjᵒ die.
C.   Itm. Margaret Atkinson doughter of Isabell Atkinson widow xped xxjᵒ die.

Aprill 1586. *Regine Eliz: 28.*

B.   Itm. George Rawson son of John Rawson buried iijᵒ die.
B.   Itm. Thomas Walker buried xxjᵒ die.
C.   Itm. John Wilie son of Will'm Wilie xped xxvjᵒ die.

May.

M.   Itm. George Crowder and Elizab. Richardson maried ijᵒ die.

June.

M. Itm. John Johnson and Mabell Stevenson maried xijᵒ die.
C. Itm. Margaret Norton a Bastard xped xvᵒ die.
M. Itm. Thomas dice and Alice Wright maried xxjᵒ die.

Julie.

M. Itm. John Bolton and An Bosse married xᵒ die.
C. Nicholas Bew son of Thomas Bew xped xvijᵒ die.
M. Itm. Anthony Johnson and Alice Corker maried xxiiijᵒ die.

August.

B. Nicholas Bew abovesaid buried xvjᵒ die.
C. Margaret Lumasse daughter of Elliseus Lumasse xped xxvᵒ die.
M. Itm. Edward dice and Margaret Bradford maried xxviijᵒ die.

September.

B. Julian Bradley wief of John Bradley buried iiijᵒ die.
B. Itm. John Skilbeck son of John Skillbeck buried viijᵒ die.

October.

B. Itm. John Turpin the elder buried jᵒ die.

November.

C. Margaret Owstabie daughter of Richard Owstabie xped jᵒ die.
B. Thomas Shippen son of John Shippen buried iijᵒ die.
C. James Armitage son of Richard Armitage xped xᵒ die.
C. Richard danniell son of Alexander danniell xped xijᵒ die.
M. Will'm Berridge and Margaret Gibson maried xxᵒ die.
C. Rob'rt Playfear son of Edmund Playfear xped xxxᵒ die.

December.

C. Will'm Scrivener son of ffraunces Scrivener xped ixᵒ die.
M. Peter Hemmingway and Margaret dean maried xjᵒ die.
B. Itm. Thomas Spinck of hillome buried xxixᵒ die.

Januarie.

B. Jane Longwood wief of John Longwood buried vᵒ die.
B. Will'm Scrivener aforesaid buried xxvjᵒ die.

Februarie.

B. Jenet Longwood wief of henry Longwood buried iiijᵒ die.
B. Elizabeth Cooke wief of thomas Cooke buried ixᵒ die.
B. Itm. John Longwood son of henry Longwood buried xiiijᵒ die.
B. Mabell Johnson wief of John Johnson buried xvjᵒ die.
B. John Shippen buried xviijᵒ die.
C. Katteren Procter doughter of Mʳ Nicolas Procter xped xviijᵒ die.
C. Margaret Wilson daughter of Rob'rt Wilson xped eadem die.
C. Rob'rt Thornton son of Edmund Thornton xped xxvjᵒ die.

March.

C. ffraunces Rawson doughter of John Rawson xped vᵒ die.

Aprill 1587. *Regine Eliz : 29.*

C. Jenet Bramham daughter of Timothy Bramham xped ijᵒ die.
C. John Browne son of Anthony Browne xped vᵒ die.
B. Will'm Berridge son of Will'm Berridge of hillome buried xᵒ die.
C. Will'm Nelson son of Will'm Nelson of the hill xped xijᵒ die.

5

May.

C.   Will'm Barmbie son of Will'm Barmbie xped xiiij° die.
C.   An Bolton daughter of John Bolton xped xxv° die.

June.

B.   Richard Collet son of Will'm Collet buried ix° die.
B.   John Dockley buried xviij° die.
C.   Thomas Morlayn son of John Morlayn xped xviij° die.

Julie.

B.   Thomas Morlayn aforesaid buried viij° die.
B.   Robert Hamond buried xxix° die.

August.

B.   Steven Nelson the son of ffraunces Nelson buried ij° die.
C.   George Hemmingway son of Ric. hemmingway xped xxvij° die.
B.   Mr Nicholas Procter minister of this parish buried xxx° die.

September.

C.   John Shippen son of James Shippen xped iij° die.
B.   Margaret Johnson wief of Oswould Johnson buried iij° die.
B.   Jane Hamond late wief of Robert hamond buried ix° die.
B.   John Shippen son of James Shippen abovesaid buried ix° die.
B.   Margaret Wilson doughter of Rob'rt Wilson buried ix° die.
B.   Isabell Gisburn widow buried xvij° die.
B.   An Shippen wief of James Shippen buried xx° die.
B.   Agnes Hemmingway widow buried xxij° die.
B.   Will'm Wells buried xxvj° die.

October.

B.   Will'm Webster buried j° die.
B.   Agnes Atkin doughter of John Atkin of Lumbie buried xviij° die.
B.   Isabell Whitley of Lumbie widow buried xx° die.

November

B.   Rob'rt Hamond son of ould Rob'rt hamond buried iij° die.
M.   Henry Turner and An Crudd maried ix° die.

December.

M.   ffraunces Scot & ursula Beamond maried ij° die.
M.   Thomas Shereburn & Margaret Bawne maried ij° die.

Januarie.

B.   John Tomson son of Edmund Playfeares wief buried xv° die.
B.   Richard Turpin buried xviij° die.
C.   Fraunces Scrivener doughter of ffraunces Scrivener xped xx° die.
M.   John Todd and Joan Robuck maried xxx° die.

Februarie.

M.   Will'm Nettleton and Katteren Richardson maried iij° die.
M.   Rob'rt Allainbrigg and Katteren bywater maried eodem die.
B.   Oswould Johnson buried iiij° die.
C.   George dannyell son of Alexander dannyell xped iiij° die.
M.   Rob'rt Wilkinson and Jane Procter maried vj° die.
B.   Katteren Procter doughter of the said Jane Procter buried xxiiij° die.

March.

C. Alice Muse doughter of Thomas Muse xped vj⁰ die.
B. Itm. Richard Pearson of hillome buried xj⁰ die.
B. ffraunces Pereson buried xiij⁰ die.
C. Thomas Hemmingway son of Peter Hemmingway xped xxij⁰ die.
C. Jenet Gilliam doughter of John Gilliam xped xxiij⁰ die.

Aprill 1588. *Regine Eliz : 30.*

B. Jenet Bywater wief of Will'm Biwater buried ij⁰ die.
C. Elizabeth Thornton doughter of Thomas Thornton xped xviij⁰ die.

May.

B. Alice Pringle servant wᵗʰ John dice buried ij⁰ die.
M. Thomas Thornton afore named and Christian Crowder maried xiiij⁰ die.
M. Thomas Watkin and dority Shippen maried xix⁰ die.
M. Rob'rt Corker and Eliz: Roundell maried xxj⁰ die.

June.

B. Anthony Carbell servant to John dice buried x⁰ die.

Julie.

B. John Fox son of Will'm ffox buried xiij⁰ die.
M. Gregory Bond and Ellen Cooke maried xiiij⁰ die.
B. Katteren Walker doughter of Jenet Walker buried xiiij⁰ die.

August.

C. James Wilburn son of James Wilburn xped xviij⁰ die.

September.

B. Henry Powthrop servant to Mʳ Wilson buried iiij⁰ die.
B. Isabell Watkin widow buried vij⁰ die.
B. Alice Bew doughter of thomas Bew buried xvij⁰ die.
C. Richard Beridge son of Robert Berridge xped xxv⁰ die.

October.

B. Rob'rt Wells Buried x⁰ die.
B. Margaret Bradforth wief of John Bradforth buried xx⁰ die.

November.

C. Elizabeth Turner doughter of henry turner xped iij⁰ die.
C. An Bramham doughter of timothy Bramham xped ix⁰ die.
C. Jane Morlay doughter of John Morlay xped ix⁰ die.
M. James Shippen and An Watkin maried xvij⁰ die.
B. Alice Simpson widow buried xxvj⁰ die.

December.

C. Rob'rt Nelson son of Will'm Nelson xped j⁰ die.
B. Hugh Coltres buried xx⁰ die.
B. Jenet Walker widow buried xxiiij die.
B. Elizabeth Harper buried xxviij⁰ die.

Januarie.

M. Rob'rt Hewit and Elizabeth Nelson maried xiiij⁰ die.
B. Edmund Playfear buried xxvj⁰ die.

Februarie.

C. Thomas Hamond son of John Hamond xped vº die.
B. John Bradforth buried xijº die.
C. An Ellison daughter of John Ellison xped xxijº die.
B. John Gilliam buried xxiiijº die.
C. dorithy Mason daughter of Thomas Mason xped xxvº die.

March.

B. Rob'rt Ward buried xvijº die.
B. An Bramham daughter of Timothy Bramham buried xxjº die.
C. Jane Lummasse doughter of Ellisse Lummas xped xxjº die.

Aprill 1589.   Regine Eliz: 31.

C. Rob'rt Bew son of thomas Bew xped xxjº die.
B. Will'm Hemmingway son of Richard hemmingway buried xxiijº die.

May.

C. Will'm dice son of John dice xped jº die.
C. Essam Norman daughter of Mʳ George Norman xped iijº die.
C. Henry Huscroft son of Henry Huscroft xped iijº die.
C. Will'm Nettleton son of Wᵐ Nettleton xped vijº die.
C. ffraunces Wilkinson daughter of Rob'rt Wilkinson xped vijº die.
C. Margaret Wilson daughter of Robert Wilson xped xxxº die.

Julie.

C. Isabell Hemmingway doughter of Richard Hemmingway xped xxjº die.

August.

B. Margaret Pereson wᶜh was the doughter of Richard Pereson buried ijº die.
C. Elizabeth Rudd daughter of Edmund Rudd xped xxxjº die.

September.

B. Margaret Ellys wief of Will'm Ellys buried iijº die.
B. Mary Woormall daughter of Mʳ John Woormall of York buried iiijº die.
B. Agnes Hutchinson wief of Richard Hutchinson buried xxº die.
B. John Hamond the eldest buried xxiiijº die.
                    October vac.

November.

B. John Hamond of hillome buried xvijº die.
M. Will'm Wells and Margaret Spinck maried xviijº die.

December.

C. Robert Turpin son of John Turpin xped vijº die.
C. An Elme daughter of Wᵐ Elm xped ixº die.

Januarie.

C. George son of Roger Norman xped xvjº die.
B. ffraunces son of Roger Norman buried eodem die.
B. An Norman wief Mʳ George Norman buried xvijº die.
B. George Norman son of the above named Roger Norman buried xixº die.
M. Anthony Watkin and An Wily maried xxvijº die.

Februarie.

M. Will'm Battell and Elizabeth Coltres married xº die.
M. Nicholas Hemmingway and Margery Parker maried xiiijº die.

B.   John Berridge son of Wm Berridge of hillome buried xv^o die.
M.   Mathew Twisleton and An Pereson maried xix^o die.
C.   Margaret Hemmingway daughter of Nicolas Hemmingway xped xxij^o die.

March.

C.   Barbara Skilbeck daughter of John Skilbeck xped vij^o die.
C.   Elizabeth Bramham doughter of timothy Bramham xped xj^o die.
C.   Alice Bolton daughter of John Bolton xped xxj^o die.

Aprill 1590. *Regine Eliz:* 32.

B.   Richard Marshall buried viij^o die.
C.   Will'm dannyell son of Alexander dannyell xped xv^o die.
B.   Richard Hutchinson buried ultimo die.

May.

C.   Elizabethe Scot doughter of ffraunces scot xped xiij^o die.

June.

B.   James Barmbow buried ij^o die.
B.   James Wilburn son of James Wilburn buried xiij^o die.
M.   Will'm Nelson Junior and Luce Middleton maried xvj^o die.

Julie.

B.   Will'm ffox buried vij^o die.
M.   Will'm Bradford and Margaret dobson maried vij^o die.
B.   Robert Drury buried xxx^o die.

August.

B.   Agnes Wauld widow buried viij^o.

September.

B.   Richard Stansfield buried xviij^o die.
C.   Alice Barmbie daughter of Will'm Barmbie xped xx^o die.

October.

C.   Margaret Scrivener doughter of ffraunces Scrivener xped xiij^o die.
B.   Agnes Gilliam wch was the doughter of John Gilliam buried xxvj^o die.
C.   Elizabethe Wells daughter of William Wells xped ultimo die.

November.

C.   Jane Wilson daughter of Mr Will'm Wilson xped j^o die.
C.   George Northen son of Andrew Northen xped j^o die.
C.   Margaret Watkin daughter of Anthony Watkin xped xxvij^o die.
B.   John Cotes buried ultimo die.
C.   Elizabethe daughter of Roger Norman xped eodem die.
C.   Nicolas Wilburn son of James Wilburn xped eodem die.

December.

B.   Robert Lawrence son of Isabell Lawrence a pore woman of Leeds buried
        xiij^o die.
B.   Alice Yeadon daughter of John Yeadon buried xvij^o die.
B.   Elizabeth Underwood widow buried xxix^o die.

Januarie.

B.   James Shippen buried xj^o die.
C.   George Berredge son of Robert Berredge xped xviij^o die.
B.   Margaret Scrivener doughter of ffraunces Scrivener buried xix^o die.

C. Will'm the bastard of John Bradford xped xxº die.
B. ffraunces Wilkinson doughter of Robert Wilkinson buried xxvº die.
B. Barbara Skilbeck doughter of John Skilbeck buried eodem die.
B. Elizabeth Lockwood a pore girle buried eodem die.
B. George Beridge before named buried xxvjº die.
M. Thomas Chambers and Ursula Robinson maried xxxº die.
B. Katteren wief of John Skilbeck buried xxxjº die.

Februarie.

B. John Skilbeck buried ijº die.
B. Isabell Cowper buried vjº die.
M. Will'm Richardson & M'gret Person maried ixº die.
B. Margaret Birom buried xixº die.

March.

B. Agnes Pereson buried ijº die.
B. Edward Jentes buried xº die.
B. George son of Alexander danyell buried eodem die.
C. Rob'rt son of Ric Hemmingway xped xiiijº die.
B. Jenet wife of thomas Bradley buried xvjº die.
B. Will'm son of Alexander danyell buried xxijº die.
B. Jenet Gilliam widow buried xxiijº die.

Aprill 1591. *Regine Eliz :* 33.

B. John Hartley buried iijº die.
B. Henry Huscroft buried xº die.
C. Will'm son of thomas Chambers xped xxº die.
B. Will'm Berridge of ffrieston buried xxviijº die.

May.

M. John Bradford & An Hodgson maried xviijº die.

June.

B. Rob'rt son of John Turpin buried vijº die.
M. Thomas Bradley & Jenet Hodson maried viijº die.

Julie.

M. Warin Walker & Jenᵗ Scrivener maried vjº die.

August.

B. Jenᵗ wief of thomas Mayson buried xxiijº die.

September.

B. Thomas Mason buried vjº die.
B. Alice doughter of John Bolton of Burton buried xvº die.

October.

C. Jane doughter of henry Roundell xped xxxº die.

November.

M. Wᵐ Hamlin and Jane Marston maried vijº die.
C. Richard son of Edmond Rud xped xxjº die.
M. Wᵐ Smith & Jenᵗ Scott maried xxviijº die.

December.

M. Robert Hartley and Isabell Cowper maried iiijº die.
B. Thomas son of George Smithies buried vº die.
B. John Turpin of ffrieston buried xº die.

B. John Barker a pore fellow buried xxiijo die.
C. doroty doughter of Nicolas hemingway xped xxiiijo die.

Januarie.

B. Will'm Elme buried ijo die.
B. Agnes Berridge buried xo die.
B. Jane wief of Rob'rt Cowper buried xo die.

Februarie.

C. Thomas son of thomas Mewse xped ijo die.
M. Rob'rt Tate and An Shippen maried vjo die.
B. ffraunces son of Mr Roger Norman buried xiijo die.
B. Margaret wief of henry Longwood buried xxiijo die.

March.

C. Dorothie Morlay xped xixo die.
B. Isabell Rawling buried xxjo die.

Aprill 1592.   *Regine Eliz:* 34.

C. ffraunces and Alice doughters of widow Elme xped xjo die.
C. George son of John Hodgeson xped xxiijo die.
B. Margery wief of Nicolas hemingway buried xxixo die.

May.

B. An wief of Alexander danyell buried xvjo die.
C. An doughter of the said dannyell xped eodem die.
M. Laurence Wilson and M'gret hamond maried xxviijo die.
C. Will'm Nelson son of Will'm Nelson Junior xped xxixo die.
C. An doughter of John Yeadon xped ultimo die.

June.

C. Elizabeth doughter of ffraunces Scrivener xped xvjo die.
C. Roger Bew son of thomas Bew xped xxvo die.
C. George son of Henry Turner xped xxviijo die.

Julie.

C. Jane doughter of Thomas Thornton xped ixo die.
B. Robert Pereson buried xxvjo die.

August.

C. An and Margaret Bond children of Gregory Bond xped ijo die.
C. dorothy Hartley doughter of Rob'rt Hartley of Burton xped xviijo die.
B. An bond abovesaid buried xixo die.
C. Elizabeth Wilson doughter of Mr Will'm Wilson xped xxvijo die.

September.

C. Richard dice son of John dice xped viijo die.
C. An doughter of Anthony Watkin xped eodem die.
C. Robert Beridge son of Rob'rt Beridge xped xiijo die.
B. Margaret Bond above said buried eodem die.
B. An doughter of Alexander dannyell buried eodem die.
C. Will'm Brown son of Launcelot Brown xped xvijo die.

October.

C. Margaret Wilkinson doughter of Robert Wilkinson xped viijo die.
B. Elizabeth Turner doughter of henry Turner buried xxijo die.
B. A pore boy (as he said) born about Leeds buried xxvjo die.

November.

B. Will'm Hallaley buried vijo die.
C. George Wells son of Wm Wells xped xvijo die.
C. Jane Bolton doughter of John Bolton xped xixo die.

December.

C. Isabell Bramham daughter of Tymothie Bramham xped iijo die.
C. Roger son of Wm Smith of Burton xped vijo die.
B. Ellen Hartley widow buried xijo die.
B. Roger Smith above said buried xixo die.

Januarie.

C. Ellen doughter of Lawrence Wilson xped ijo die.
C. Margaret daughter of John Bradford xped xxvo die.
C. Richard son of Anthony Browne xped eodem die.
C. Christopher son of Wm Bradford xped xiiijo die ffebruarii.
M. Will'm Berridge and Agnes Elme maried xxjo die ffebruarii.
C. An doughter of Ellis Lumas xped ultimo die ffebruarii.

March.

C. Margaret Bradley doughter of thomas Bradley xped xxjo die.

Anno d'ni : 1593. Regine Eliz : 35.

C. Robert son of George Atkinson xped xxxo die.
B. Margaret Bradley above said buried ultimo die.
B. Alexander Shippen buried eodem die.

Aprill.

B. Xpopher Patrick a servant buried vijo die.
B. Elizabeth wief of George Crowther buried xijo die.
B. An doughter of Anthony Watkin buried xxiijo die.

May.

B. An Tate wief Robert Tate buried viijo die.
M. Nicolas hemmingway & ffraunces Lakeland maried xxixo die.
                                      Junius vac.

Julie.

M. Thomas Clark & Elizabeth hodgson maried iijo die.
M. Alexander dannyell & Jen^t Turpin maried xo die.
M. Rob'rt Howdell & Ellen Gurlick maried xvo die.
C. Margery Grannt xped xxijo die.

August.

B. Richard Browne son of Anthony Browne buried xxixo die.

September.

B. George son of Ric. hemingway buried xjo die.
B. Alexander danyel buried xxjo die.
C. Wm Laycock the son of Jenet laycock being a bastard xped eodem die.

October.

B. Thomas Kitchin buried vjo die.
M. John Haslewood and Agnes Park maried xiiijo die.
B. Luce Nelson wief of Will'm Nelson buried xxxjo die.
C. Margaret Nelson doughter of the sd. Wm Nelson xped eodem die.

November.

M. Will'm Bolton and Barbara Marshall maried xijᵒ die.
M. Robert Marshall and Elizabeth Parker maried xviijᵒ die.
M. Hugh Richardson and Mary Calbeck maried xxvᵒ die.

December.

C. Rob'rt Bond son of Gregorie Bond xped xiijᵒ die.

Januarie.

C. Margaret Turner doughter of Henry Turner xped xvjᵒ die.

ffebruarie.

C. John Roundell son of Henry Roundell xped xxjᵒ die.
C. ffraunces Clark son of Thomas Clark xped eodem die.
B. Will'm Scot son of Robert Scot buried xxiijᵒ die.
C. Margaret Haslewood doughter of John Haslewood xped xxvijᵒ die.

March.

B. Isabell Webster widow buried iijᵒ die.
B. Jane Browne buried xᵒ die.
C. Katteren Wells doughter of Wᵐ Wells xped xiijᵒ die.
C. Alexander Norman son of Mʳ Roger Norman xped xvjᵒ die.

Aprill 1594: *Regine Eliz:* 36.

C. Richard hemingway son of Nicolas Hemmingway xped xvjᵒ die.
C. Margret Smith doughter of Wᵐ Smith of Burton xped xxviijᵒ die.

May.

C. Margret Rud doughter of Edmund Rud xped xxᵒ die.
B. Margret doughter of John Haslewood buried xxjᵒ die.
C. ffraunces doughter of Robert Howdell xped xxvjᵒ die.

June.

C. ffraunces Longwood doughter of Henry Longwood of Burton xped ijᵒ die.
M. John Spinck and Katteren Rayner maried xxvᵒ die.

Julie.

M. John Hasleby and Elizabeth Ellys maried xiiijᵒ die.
B. Mary Northen doughter of Andrew Northen buried xvᵒ die.

August.

C. Katteren doughter of Warin Walker of Stillingfleet xped xxiiijᵒ die.

September.

C. ffraunces Northen doughter of Andrew Northen xped jᵒ die.
C. Alice Scrivener doughter of ffraunces Scrivener xped jᵒ die.
B. & An Scrivener wief of ffraunces Scrivener buried iiijᵒ die.
M. Wᵐ Nelson and Jane Waterson maried xᵒ die.
C. Jane doughter of Wᵐ Beridge of Burton xped xxixᵒ die.
C. Arthure son of thomas Chambers xped eodem die.

October.

C. Elizabeth Bradford doughter of John Bradford xped vjᵒ die.
M. Arthure Johnson and Mary Harrison maried vjᵒ die.
B. Henry Mitton buried xxixᵒ die.

6

November.

B.   Isabell Cotes widow buried iiijo die.
M.   Wm Bellabie and Jenet dannyell maried xo die.
B.   Agnes Howdell widow buried xxviijo die.

December.

C.   Jent Marcer doughter of John Marcer xped viijo die.
C.   John Beridge son of Robert Beridge xped xvo die.
C.   George Hemingway son of Richard Hemingway xped xxvjo die.

Januarie.

B.   Richard Turner buried iiijo die.
C.   George Bramham xped vo die.
C.   ffraunces Watkin son of Anthony watkin xped xixo die.
B.   Thomas Muse son of Thomas Muse buried xxvijo die.

ffebruarie.

B.   Alice Eliot widow buried iiijo die.
B.   Margaret Wilkinson daughter of Robert Wilkinson buried vo die.
M.   John Browne and Margaret Morlayn maried xjo die.

March.

C.   Will'm Richardson son of Hugh Richardson xped ixo die.
C.   Margaret Robinson doughter of Edward Robinson xped xvjo die.

Anno D'ni 1595 : *Regine Eliz :* 37.

B.   Jane wief to Richard Laycock buried xxixo die Martii.

Aprill.

B.   Will'm Biwater buried ijo die.
C.   ffraunces Hartley daughter of Robert Hartley xped vjo die.
B.   Grace Northen wief of Andrew Northen buried vjo die.
C.   Jent doughter of John Haslewood xped xxvijo die.

May.

C.   George Wharledayle and ffraunces Wharledayle sons of Brian Wharledayl
       xped xxiiijo die.

June.

C.   Elizabeth Spinck daughter of John Spinck xped jo die.
B.   John Hasleybie buried ijo die.
C.   John Loft son of Nicolas Loft xped viijo die.
C.   An Nelson doughter of Wm Nelson Junior xped viijo die.
C.   Isabell Hasleybie daughter of Elizabeth Hasleybie widow xped xxijo die.
B.   Robert Benbow buried xxvo die.
C.   George Bew son of Thomas Bew xped xxixo die.

Julie.

B.   Margaret Bradford doughter of John Bradford buried iijo die.
B.   Elizabeth Spinck abovesaid buried eodem die.
B.   An Nelson abovesaid buried eodem die.
C.   Edward Bolton son of Wm Bolton xped xxo die.

August.

C.   Elizabeth Wilkinson daughter of Robert Wilkinson xped xo die.
C.   Jenet Brown daughter of Elizabeth Brown a widow which late came from
       Blithe xped eodem die.

B. Agnes Mitton widow buried xiij° die.
B. Agnes Hartley of Burton buried xiiij° die.

Septemb: vac.

October.

M. Robert Butler and Katteren Hartley maried xix° die.
M. Richard Gilliam and Margaret Hamond maried xxviij° die.

November.

M. John Walker and Elizabeth Huscroft maried ij° die.
C. dorothy Graunger xped xvj° die.
C. Will'm the Bastard of Edward Procter xped xxx° die.

December.

C. Margaret Johnson xped vij° die.
B. Elizabeth Wilie Widow buried xiiij° die.
B. Thomas Bradley buried xxix° die.

Januarie.

C. Jane Bradford daughter of Wᵐ Bradford xped j° die.

ffebruarie.

B. John Pereson buried x° die.

March.

C. B. John Lumby xped vij° die and buried ix° die.
B. An Smithe Widow buried xvj° die.
C. Jenet Browne daughter of Launcelot Brown xped xxj° die.

Aprilis vac.

May 1596: Regine Eliz: 38.

B. Will'm Beridge of Hillome buried xix° die.
C. Rob'rt Spinck son of John Spinck xped xx° die.

June.

C. Agnes daughter of John bolton of Burton xped j° die.
B. George son of henry Turner buried iij° die.
C. Will'm Turner son of the said henry turner xped vj° die.
C. Jenet Burton daughter of John Burton xped vj° die.
C. Katteren doughter of Wᵐ Nelson Junior xped xxvij° die

Julie.

C. John Pereson son of Elizabethe Pereson of hillome widow late wief of John
     Pereson deceased xped iiij° die therefore yᵉ said Jo: Pereson was 40 yeares
     of age compleat the 17ᵗʰ of July before he dyed wh. was in the yeare of o'r
     Lo: 1636.
B. ffraunces Playfere widow buried v° die.

August.

C. ffraunces Grannt daughter of thomas Grannt xped j° die.

September.

B. Agnes Bolton daughter of Joh. Bolton buried ij° die.
B. Robert Spinck son of John Spinck buried xij° die.
C. Katteren Harrison doughter of one John Harrison a Strannger xped xix° die.
C. Christofer son of Nicolas hemmingway xped eodem die.

October.

C. ffraunces son of gregory Bond xped iijᵒ die.
C. Thomas Roundell son of Henry Roundell xped xᵒ die.
M. John Ellys and Kateren Nelson maried eodem die.
B. ffraunces Bond abovesaid buried xvjᵒ die.
C. George Gilliam son of Richard Gilliam xped xxxjᵒ die.

November.

M. John Battell & Jenet Bradley maried vijᵒ die.
C. Agnes Clark doughter of thomas Clark xped eodem die.
C. An Walker doughter of ffraunces Walker of Stillingfleete xped xiiijᵒ die.
C. George son of Edmund Rud xped xvijᵒ die.
M. Robert Spinck & Elizabeth Pereson maried xxiijᵒ die.
B. An Walker abovesaid buried xxvᵒ die.

December.

B. ffraunces Wharledayle buried xvᵒ die.
B. Gilbert Northen buried xxᵒ die.

Januarie.

C. ffraunces Mitton xped xvjᵒ die.
C. Christofer son of Richard Hemmingway xped xxiijᵒ die.

ffebruarie.

B. Margret wief of Antony Brown buried vjᵒ die.
C. Rob'rt Wells son of Wᵐ Wells xped vjᵒ die.
B. Isabell Beridge buried xᵒ die.

March.

B. ffraunces Grannt buried iijᵒ die.
B. An doughter of george Smith buried xvjᵒ die.
B. Margret wief of Rob'rt Scot buried xvijᵒ die.
B. Christofer hemingway buried xxᵒ die.
C. Isabell Vevers xped xxᵒ die.

Aprill 1597 Regine Eliz : 39.

B. dorothie Mason buried vᵒ die.
B. Isabell vevers buried vijᵒ die.
B. John Smith buried xvᵒ die.
C. Thomas Berridge son of Robert Berridge xped xxiiijᵒ die.

May.

C. Thomas Spinck son of John Spinck xped jᵒ die.
B. Margret Hemmingway widow buried ijᵒ die.
C. George son of henry Longwood xped xvᵒ die.
C. Ellen doughter of Robert Butler xped xvᵒ die.

June.

B. John Leaper buried xviijᵒ die.

Julius vac.

August.

B. Mʳ Robert Elam minister here buried vjᵒ die.
C. Jane Ellys doughter of John Ellis xped vijᵒ die.
B. Will'm Bramham buried xvᵒ die.
B. Richard ffearnley buried xxvjᵒ die.

September.

C. Will'm Norman son of Mr George Norman xped xxv^o die.

October.

B. Agnes Clark doughter of thomas Clark buried iij^o die.
B. ffraunces Hartley buried eodem die.
B. Jen^t Smith widow buried xiij^o die.
C. John Lumby son of Mathew Lumby xped xvj^o die.
B. John Roundell buried xx^o die.
C. Jane Bradford doughter of John Bradford xped xx^o die.
B. Thomas Burnby buried xxiij^o die.
B. George Englot buried xxiiij^o die.
M. Richard Clark and Jane hodgson maried xxvj^o die.

November.

M. Thomas Lawrence & Margret Nicolson maried v^o die.
B. Elizabeth Longwood buried xj^o die.
C. ffraunces doughter of henry Rodins xped xxiiij^o die.
M. Thomas Leathom and Elizabeth Mowton maried xxvj^o die.
B. Isabel doughter of Richard Hemmingway buried xxix^o die.
C. Jen^t Bolton doughter of John Bolton xped xxx^o die.
B. ffraunces Rodons abovesaid buried xxx^o die.
C. Edward Scrivener son of Frannces Scrivener of Hambleton was xped in the Parish Church of Brayton xxx^o die Novembris, 1597.

December.

B. Robert son of Will'm Wells buried ix^o die.
C. Alice Robinson daughter of Edward Robinson xped xj^o die.
B. Jen^t doughter of John Burton buried eodem die.
B. dorothy Wauld wief of George Wauld buried xix^o die.
B. Will'm Wauld son of the said George Wauld buried xx^o die.
B. Isabell Turner widow buried xxvj^o die.
B. John Norman, gent., buried xxix^o die.

Januarie.

B. Elizabeth Walker wief to Jo: Walker buried v^o die.
B. Isabell Nelson wief to Wm Nelson senior buried vj^o die.
B. John Yeadon buried xv^o die.
B. Will'm Bradford buried eodem die.
B. An Hartley widow buried xviij^o die.
B. Ralf Swan buried xxj^o die.
B. Rob'rt Playfear buried xxix^o die.
B. Mary Cowper buried eodem die.
B. Will'm Sharphowse buried xxxj^o die.

ffebruarie.

M. John Johnson and Julian Laycock maried vij^o die.
M. John Pereson & Susan Wilkinson maried eodem die.
B. Agnes Spiser buried xviij^o die.
B. An Smith doughter to Ric. Smith of Brighton buried xxv^o die.

March.

C. John Bew son of thomas Bew xped iij^o die.
B. Isabell wief to Xpofer Wilson buried iiij^o die.
B. Isabell doughter of Wm Hamond buried eodem die.
B. Wm Beridge of Burton buried vj^o die.

B. George Rud son of Edmund Rud buried xvº die.
B. Alice Beridge Widow buried xxijº die.

Anno D'ni 1598 : *Regine Eliz :* 40.

B. Elizabeth Spinck widow buried xxxº die. Martii.

Aprill.

C. Roger Northen son of Andrew Northen xped ijº die.
C. Jane doughter of Nicolas Hemingway xped ijº die.
B. Christopher Bellabie servant to Jo: Bradford buried vº die.
B. John Morlay buried xº die.
B. Agnes Crowder widow buried xjº die.
B. Robert Salmon buried xvº die.

May.

B. Will'm Ellys buried iijº die.
B. Agnes Ward widow buried vº die.

June.

C. George Lummas son of Ellis Lummas xped xjº die.
M. Nicolas Wauld and ffraunces Morlay maried xiijº die.
C. Will'm Spinck son of John Spinck xped xiijº die.
C. Henry Oldfeild son of Thomas Oldfeild xped xxixº die.

Julie.

C. Edward Gilliam son of Ric. Gilliam xped xº die.

August.

C. Katteren Chambers doughter of thomas Chambers xped vjº die.
C. Richard Richardson son of Hughe Richardson xped eod vjº die.
M. Simon Kirkby and Ellen Clough maried xxº day.
C. Mary Beridge doughter of widow Beridge of Burton xped eod die.
B. Edward Gilliam above said buried xxijº die.
B. Agnes Hallaley born in Burton buried xxiiijº die.

September.

C. John Illingwoorth xped iijº die.
C. Thomas Hartley xped eod iijº die.
C. Wᵐ Bradford son of M'gret Bradford widow xped xxº die.

October.

B. Richard Richardson aforesaid buried vijº die.
M. Rich. Bowling Minister here and Margaret Morlay maried xvjº die.
C. B. Richard Bond xped xviijº die and buried xxvjº die.
C. Mary Nelson doughter of Wᵐ Nelson Junior xped xxviijº die.

November.

C. Margret Wells doughter of Wᵐ Wells xped vjº die.
M. Thomas Leaper and Elizabeth King maried xjº die.
B. Thomas Shereburn buried xvjº die.
C. George Norman son of Mʳ George Norman xped xixº die.
C. ffraunces Johnson son of Ric. Johnson xped xxvº die.
C. Will'm Laycock son of Wᵐ Laycock xped xxxº die.

December.

M. Robert Shan and Margret Bradford maried xijº die.
C. ffraunces Turner xped xxjº die.

C. Thomas Watkin xped xxj⁰ die.
B. Jen^t Leaper widow buried xxv⁰ die.

Januarie.

C. Margret Bramham xped vj⁰ die.
M. Mr Will'm Wilson & Mrs Bridget Oglethorp maried viij⁰ die.
C. Elizabeth and Ann Ward Twinnes xped xxvij⁰ die. ,

ffebruariea.

C. Alice Spinck doughter of Rob'rt Spinck xped ij⁰ die.
C. Richard Clark xped vj⁰ die.
C. Nicholas Leathom xped x⁰ die.
C. Will'm Vevers xped xvj⁰ die.
B. Elizabeth Ward above said buried xxvij⁰ die.

March.

B. Will'm Bond son of Gregory Bond buried xiij⁰ die.

Anno D'ni 1599: *Regine Eliz :* 41.

B. Margery Bolton wief of tho: Bolton of Burton buried xxx⁰ die.

Aprill.

M. George ffoyster and Alice Stansfeild maried ultimo die.

May.

M. John Walker & Elizabeth Stansfeld maried viij⁰ die.
B. George Longwood buried x⁰ die.
B. ffraunces Scrivener doughter of ffraunces Scrivener buried xvj⁰ die.
C. Elizabeth doughter of Arthure Johnson xped xx⁰ die.
C. Robert Valentine xped xxvij⁰ die.
C. Isabell Pereson doughter of John Pereson xped xxvij⁰ die.

June.

C. Rob'rt haslewood xped xxiiij⁰ die.
C. Thomas Burton xped eodem xxiiij⁰ die.

Julie.

C. Isabell Rud xped xxix⁰ die.

August.

C. xpofer Spinck son of John Spinck xped xix⁰ die.

September.

C. An Gilliam doughter of Richard Gilliam xped xx⁰ die.
C. Richard Ellys son of John Ellys xped xxiij⁰ die.

October.

C. Robert Shan xped vij⁰ die.
B. An Salmon widow buried xiij⁰ die.
M. John Howdell and Bridget Illingwoorthe maried xvj⁰ die.
C. Elizabeth Wilson doughter of Christofer Wilson of Hillom xped xxvij⁰ die.

November.

C. Roger Becket son of Richary Becket of Burton xped xiij⁰ die.
M. Robert Wilson and Agnes Snawden maried xviij⁰ die.
B. M^ris An Norman wief of Mr Thomas Norman of Gateforth buried xxij⁰ die.
M. John diconson and Elizabeth Asleyby maried xxv⁰ die.

December

C. Marie Waulde doughter of Nicholas Waulde of ffrieston xped iijᵒ die.

B. ffraunces ffoyster a Young Infant being the son of George ffoyster of Burton buried xᵒ die.

C. Mary Roundell doughter of Henry Roundell of ffrieston xped xxvjᵒ die.

Januarie.

C. Margaret Scroop a Bastard whose ffather is not knowne being doughter to An Scroope Vagrant Beggar xped vjᵒ die.

B. A child not xped being doughter of Christopher Sayner of hillome buried xvjᵒ die.

C. Will'm Rodehowse son of Henry Rodous of ffrieston xped xxijᵒ die.

M. Richard dussan and Isabell Ellis maried xxvijᵒ die.

ffebruarie.

C. Mary Leaper doughter of thomas Leaper of hillome xped ijᵒ die.

B. John Ledsham son of Fraunces Ledsham of Hambleton xped at Brayton Church xxvijᵒ die Februarii 1599.

C. dorithie Richardson doughter of Hugh Richardson of ffrieston xped xxvᵒ die.

      Martius vac.

Aprill 1600 : anno Regine Eliz : 42ᵒ.

B. Elizabeth Crud wife of Will'm Crud of Hillome Buried iijᵒ die.

C. John Chamber son of Thomas Chamber of Hillome xped vjᵒ die.

May.

C. Margaret Wilson doughter of Mʳ Will'm Wilson junior xped xiijᵒ die 1600 ut supra.

June.

C. Jane Richardson doughter of Wᵐ Richardson of ffrieston dwelling at the West end of the towne xped jᵐᵒ die.

C. Richard Bradforth son of John Bradforth of Hillome xped vjᵒ die.

C. Mary Berridge and Alice Berridge doughters of Robert Berridge of ffrieston xped vijᵐᵒ die.

Julie.

C. Isabell Robinson doughter of Edward Robinson of Hillom xped xxᵐᵒ die.

C. Will'm Bond and Thomas Bond sons of Gregory Bond of ffrieston xped xxxᵐᵒ die.

August.

C. Jane Rhodes doughter of Brian Rhodes of Burton xped xᵐᵒ die.

C. John Spinck and Elizabeth Spinck children of John Spinck of hillom xped ultimo die.

September.

C. Isabell Butler doughter of Robert Butler of Hillom xped vijᵐᵒ die.

C. Robert Walker son of John Walker of ffrieston xped xijᵒ die.

C. Margaret Bedall doughter of John Bedall of ffrieston xped xvᵒ die.

C. Mary Northen doughter of Andrew Northen of Burton xped xxjᵐᵒ die.

C. George Howdell son of John Howdell of Burton xped xxiiijᵒ die.

B. Richard Hemmingway son of Richard Hemmingway of hillome xped xxviijᵐᵒ die.

October.

B. Isabell West of hillom widow buried vijᵐᵒ die.

C. Jenet Lumbie doughter of Mathewe Lumbie of ffrieston xped xxvjᵐᵒ die.

November.

John Norman son of Mr George Norman of Burton xped ij⁰ die.
Thomas Smith and M'gret Muse maried xj^{mo} die.
George Howdel son of John Howdel of Burton buried xxj^{mo} die.
Will'm Boak son of Isabell Boak remayneing wth Thomas Heiforth of hillome
   xped xxvj^{mo} die.

december.

Richard Lummas son of Elias Lummas xped x^{mo} die.
John Norman son of Mr George Norman buried xij⁰ die.
Bridget Clark doughter of Thomas Clark of ffrieston xped xxvij^{mo} die.

Januarie.

Christopher dannyell son of W^m dannyell of Steeton in Shereburn pishe xped
   iiij⁰ die.
Richard Hemmingway son of Richard Hemmingway above said buried xij^{mo}
   die.
Will'm Cloice a pore lame man travailing from Gilling to the Bathe died at
   Monkfrieston and was there buried xxvij^{mo} die.
Richard Lapidge and ffraunces Ashton maried xxix⁰ die.

ffebruarius vacat.

March.

Mary Browne doughter of Launcelet Brown of ffrieston xped iiij^{to} die.
Richard Ellysse son of John Ellys of ffrieston buried v⁰ die.
Margaret Bolton doughter of John Boulton of Burton xped viij⁰ die.
Alice Tutill doughter of thomas Tutill of Burton xped xxij^{mo} die.

Anno d'ni 1601 : Regine Elizabethe : 43.

John Crosland son of Peter Crosland of ffrieston xped xxix^{mo} die.

Aprill.

ffraunces Pereson doughter of John Pereson of ffriston xped xj⁰ die.
Jane Richardson of Burton buried xvij⁰ die.
An Wells doughter of Wm Wells of hillom xped xix^{mo} die.
Isabell Hill doughter of Thomas Hill of hillom xped eodem die.

Maius vac.

June.

Richard Hemmingway of Hillome buried viij⁰.
Will'm Nettleton of Hillome buried xiij⁰ die.
Richard Vevers son of Will'm Vevers of hillome xped xv⁰ die.
Bridget Middlewood doughter of John Middlewood of ffrieston xped xxij⁰ die.

Julie.

Margret Norman doughter of Mr Roger Norman of Burton xped viij⁰ die.
Thoms ffoyster son of George ffoyster of Burton xped xv⁰ die.

August.

John Ward son of Will'm Ward of Hillom xped iiij^{to} die.
George Spinck son of Rob'rt Spinck of hillome xped xiij^{mo} die.
Bridget Gilliam doughter of Richard Gilliam of hillome xped xvij^{mo} die.
Thomas dobson son of Rob'rt dobson of ffrieston xped xxx^{mo} die.

September.

Margaret Belton doughter of thomas Bolton of Burton xped xiij^{mo} die.
Elizabeth Nelson doughter of John Nelson of Monckfrieston xped xv^{mo} die.
John diconson of ffryston buried xxiij^{mo} die.

October vacat.

November.

C. Godfrey Spinck son of John Spinck of hillome xped xiiij° die.
B. Thomisin Wilbarne wief of James Wilbarne of ffrieston buried xv° die.

December.

C. John Bond son of Gregorie Bond of ffrieston xped xiij° die.
C. Alice Norman Doughter of Mr George Norman xped xv° die.

Januarie.

C. Priscilla ffletcher doughter of John ffletcher the younger of ffrieston xped xiiij° die.
B. Richard Gilliam of Hillom Husbandman buried xxv^{mo} die.
C. George Wauld son of Nicholas Wauld of frieston xped xxvj° die.
C. Thomas Ellysse son of John Ellysse of ffrieston xped xxxj^{mo} die.

ffebruarie.

M. Brian Cuningham and Martha Banister maried j^{mo} die.
B. Jenet Benbow of Hillome buried eodm die.
M. Edward Wilson and Elizabethe diconson maried iiij° die.
B. Richard Lumby son of Mathew Lumby buried eodm die.
B. Thomas Ellysse abovesaid buried xv° die.
B. Alice ffoyster wief of George ffoyster buried xvij^{mo} die.
C. Anne Shan daughter of Rob'rt Shan of ffrieston xped eod. die.
B. Alice Elme of Burton buried xxij° die.
C. John Leathome son of Thomas Leathome of ffrieston xped xxiij° die.
B. Widow Staynsfeild of Burton buried xxviij° die.

March.

B. Rob'rt Hartley of Burton buried v° die.
B. Dorithie Hartley doughter of the said Rob'rt Hartley buried vij° die.

Aprill, 1602. anno Regine Eliz : 44.

B. Henry Longwood of Burton buried ix° die.
B. Henry Rodehowse of ffrieston buried xiiij° die.

May.

C. Nicholas Berredge son of Rob'rt Berredge of ffrieston xped xiij° die.
B. Richard Spoforth of Hillome buried xxvj° die.
C. Bridget Johnson doughter of Arthure Johnson of Hillom xped xxx^{mo} die.

June.

B. Fraunces Scrivener buried 14mo die.
C. Robert Leaper son of Thomas Leaper of hillom xped xxiiij° die.
C. John West son of James West of hillom xped eod. die.
Julius vacat.

August.

B. Elizabethe Backhowse of ffrieston buried xiiijth die.

September.

B. Richard Gilliam of Hillom laborer buried xv° die.
B. Alice Norman Doughter of Mr George Norman of Burton buried xxiij° die.

October.

M. Rob'rt Palmer and Elizabethe wharldayle married xij^{mo} die.

November.

M. Edward Wells and Margaret Shippen maried iiijto die.
C. Elsabethe Hill doughter of Thomas Hill of Hillome xped vijmo die.
B. Jenet Smithe daughter of John Smithe of Burton buried xxiijo die.
C. John Nelson son of John Nelson of ffrieston xped xxviijo die.

December.

B. Isabell Pearson of hillome widow buried ijo die.
C. Elsabeth Norman daughter of Mr George Norman of Burton xped vo die.
B. Dorithie Berredge wief of Rob'rt Berredge of ffrieston buried vjo die.
C. Margett Sayner daughter of xþofer Sayn' of Hillom xped xixo die.

Januarie.

B. Margret Willson wief of Lawrence Willson of ffrieston buried xiijo die.
C. Elizabeth Robinson daughter of Edward Robinson of hillom xped xxiiijo die.
C. ffraunces Howdell doughter of John Howdell of Burton xped eodem die.
B. Thomas diconson of ffrieston buried xxvijo die.

ffebruarie.

B. George Norman son of Mr George Norman buried ijo die.
C. Marie Willson daughter of Mr Will'm Willson junior xped viijo die.
C. Marie Watkin Daughter of Anthonie Watkin xped ixo die ffebru.
B. Bridget Johnson doughter of Arthure Johnson buried xvjo.

Marche.

C. Will'm Ellysse son of John Ellysse xped vo die.
C. ffraunces Dussan daughter of Richard dussan xped xiijmo die.

Aprill 1603. anno Regis Jacobi & jmo

C. Jane Bond doughter of Gregorie Bond xped jmo die.
C. Jenet Ouldroyd daughter of Thomas Ouldroyd xped xxijo die.
C. Marie Bedall daughter of John Beadall xped die p'dcto viz. 22.
B. Margaret Willson doughter of Mr Will'm Willson junior buried xxvo die.

May.

B. Katharine ffox widow buried jmo die.
C. Margaret Spinck daughter of John Spinck of hillom xped vjo die.
B. Margaret Spinck above said buried xiijo die.
B. ffraunces Bedall wief of John Bedall buried xiiijto die.
B. Jane Bond doughter of Gregory Bond buryed xxmo die.
M. Will'm Woodhowse and Elizabeth Hamond maried xxiijo die.

June.

M. John Johnson and Jane Rodehowse married vo die.
C. Francis Nelson son of Will'm Nelson xped xijmo die in the parish Church of Addingham.

Julie.

B. Elizabethe Nelson doughter of John Nelson of frieston buried xviijo die.
C. Eupham Bolton doughter of John Bolton of Burton xped xxiiijo die.
B. Edward Procter of frieston buried xxiiijo die.
B. John Nelson son of John Nelson of frieston buried xxiiijo die.
B. Robert Rayner of Hillom buried xxvjo die.
B. Dorothy Richardson daughter of Hughe Richardson buried xxixo die.
C. Hughe Pigot a Bastard son of Margret Pigot begotten as she sayeth by Michaell Harrison an hostler dwelling wth one Mr ffroome in London near newgate att the signe of the seriante Head xped xxxjmo die.

August.

C. Edward Wells son of Will'm Wells of Hillom xped v⁰ die.
B. Thomas Waulsh of Burton buried vij^mo die.
M. Robert ffeild and Margaret Gilliam married viij⁰ die.

September.

M. John Wilkinson and Isabell Hartley maried xxv⁰ die.
C. Mabell Cressee doughter of Mr Everingham Cressee Esquirer xped at rest park xxv⁰ die.

October.

C. Robert Wells son of Edward Wells of Hillom xped xiiij⁰ die.

November.

B. An Bradford wief of John Bradford of Hillom buried vj⁰ die.
C. Agnes Cuningham doughter of Mr Brian Cuningham xped xx⁰ die.
M. Will'm Tomlinson and Eupham Maskall maried eodem die.
M. Will'm Tayler and Elizabeth Hunter maried xxiiij⁰ die.
B. John Bradford of Hillom buried xxix⁰ die.

December.

C. Alexander Tutill son of Thomas Tutill of Burton xped iij⁰ die.
B. George Smythies of Hillom buried iiij^to die.
B. Jenet Wray wief of George Wray of Hillom buried x⁰ die.
B. Elizabeth Dice wief of Robert Dice of Hillom buried xj^mo die.
B. John Boulton of Burton buried xxvj^to die.
B. Rob'rt dice of Hillom buried xxix⁰ die.

Januarie.

B. Eupham Boulton doughter of Widow Boulton of Burton buried xv⁰ die.
C. Mary Dobson doughter of Robert dobson of Monkefrieston xped xvj⁰ die.
C. Alice Norman doughter of Mr Roger Norman of Burton xped xix⁰ die.

ffebruary.

C. William Browne son of Mr Cuthbert Browne of Lumby w^tin the Parish of Shereburne xped ij⁰ die.
M. John Beedall and Suzanna Burton maried iiij^to die.
C. Edmund Lapidge xped xij⁰ die.

March.

C. William Wilson son of Mr William Wilson junior xped at Rawden in Guyseley parish j^mo die.
C. Robert Spynck son of Robert Spinck of Hyllom xped xj^mo die.
C. John Barmbowe son of John Barmbowe of ffrieston xped xxj^mo die.

Aprill 1604 anno Regis Jacobi secundo.

B. Robert Scot of Burton buried iij⁰ die.
C. Elizabeth Smythies doughter of Edithe Smythies of Hillome being (as she affirmethe) bastard to Will'm Palmer of Coates xped xiiij^th die.
C. John Clark son of Thomas Clarke of frieston xped xv⁰ die.
C. Nicolas Crosland son of Peter Crosland of frieston xped xv⁰ die.
C. Elizabethe ffeild doughter of Robert ffeild of Hillom xped xxix⁰ die.

May.

C. Thomas Ward son of Will'm Ward of Hillom xped xiij⁰ die.
B. Twoe young Infants a son and a Doughter children of Rob'rt Berredge of Monkfrieston buried xiij⁰ die.

B.   Ellyn Berredge wief of the said Robert Berredge buried xvijᵒ die.
B.   Margaret Nelson of ffrieston buried xxiijᵒ die.
C.   Thomas Shan son of Rob'rt Shan of frieston xped xxv die.

June.

B.   Mary Beedall daughter of John Beedall buried xvj die.
C.   Alice Northen doughter of Andrewe Northen of Burton xped xixᵒ die.

July.

B.   Thomas Ward son of Will'm Ward of Hillom buried iijᵒ die.
C.   An Spinck doughter of John Spinck of Hillom xped vᵒ die.
C.   Richard Shippen son of Will'm Shippen of Hillom xped viijᵒ die.
C.   James Roundeyll son of Henry Roundell of frieston xped xxvᵒ die.
C.   John ffletcher son of John ffletcher junior of frieston xped xxixᵒ die.

August.

B.   Jenet Roundeyll wief of Henry Roundeyll of frieston buried ijᵒ die.
B.   George Waulde of frieston buried the same daye.

September.

C.   Jane Johnson doughter of Arthure Johnson of hillom xped ijᵒ die.

                                   Richard Bowling.
                                   Will'm Nelson.

B.   John Hambleton a scottish man buried in Lumby layne xᵒ die.
B.   Thomas Beredge son of Rob'rt Beredge of frieston died of the plague eod. xᵒ die.
B.   Cicilie Beredge wief of the said Rob'rt Beredge died of the plagu xjᵒ die.
B.   John Berredge son of the said Rob'rt Beredge died of the plagu xijᵒ die.
C.   Mathew Bolton son of Thomas Bolton of Burton xped xxjᵐᵒ die.
B.   Nicholas Berredge son of the said Rob'rt Berredge and Alice dixon his maide died of the plagu xxiiijᵒ die.

October.

C.   Jane Rawlinson doughter of Rob'rt Rawlinson of frieston xped xᵒ die.
B.   Isabell Wilson servant to Lawrence Wilson of frieston died of the plague xiijᵒ die.
B.   ffraunces Turner doughter of Henry Turner of frieston died of the plague eodem xiijᵒ die.
B.   Margaret Turner doughter of the said Henry Turner died of the plagu xiiijᵒ die.
B.   An Turner wief of the said Henry Turner died of the plagu xvijᵒ die.
B.   Henry Turner above said died of the plagu xixᵒ die.
B.   Ellen Willson doughter of Lawrence Willson above said died of the plagu eodem xixᵒ die.
B.   An Shan doughter of Rob'rt Shan of frieston died of the plagu xxijᵒ die.
B.   Elizabeth Awmond doughter in law to Lawrence wilson abovesd. died of the plagu xxiijᵒ die.
B.   Thomas Mearbeck prentice to Henry Turner abovesd. died of the plagu xxvijᵒ die.
B.   Will'm Turner son of the sd. Henry Turner died of the plagu xxviijᵒ die.

November.

C.   Isabell doughter of hughe Richardson of frieston xped jᵐᵒ die.
B.   Lawrence Wilson above said dyed of the plagu vᵒ die.

B. Jane Rawlinson abovesd. was buried xxjᵐᵒ die.
C. Dorothie Wauld daughter of Nicholas Wauld of frieston xped xxjᵐᵒ die.
M. Will'm Baker and Eupham Rymington maried xxijᵒ die.
C. Will'm son of Rob'rt Buttler of hillom xped xxvᵒ die.
B. Robert Shan son of Rob'rt Shan abovesd. dyed of the plagu xxvᵒ die.

December.

M. Will'm Burinton? and An . . . . . William Simson and An Wilton? maryed jᵐᵒ
die.

Richard Bowling.
Will'm Nelson.

B. Rob'rt Shan of frieston dyed of the plagu ijᵒ die.
B. Thomas Shan son of the sd. Rob'rt Shan dyed of the plagu xixᵒ die.
C. John Bedall son of John beedall of frieston xped xxjᵐᵒ die.
B. Christopher Bradford late son of Will'm Bradford of frieston dyed of the
plague xxiiijᵒ die.
B. Christian Diconson of frieston widow dyed of the plagu eod. die.

Januarius vacat.

ffebruarie.

B. John Clark son of Thomas Clark of frieston buried vᵒ die.
C. Katherin doughter of John Ellysse of frieston xped xᵒ die.
C. Margaret doughter of John Brown of frieston xped xvᵒ die.

Marche.

B. Alexander Norman son of Mʳ George Norman of Burton buried iijᵒ die.
Will'm Crudde of Hillom was found hanged in a kerchief on a gallow balk
wᵗhin his owne dwellinghowse there wᵗhin the chymney being found by
the inquest guilty of his owne deathe xixᵒ die.
B. ffraunces Clark son of Thomas Clarck of frieston dyed of the plague xxijᵒ die.
B. Richard Clark son of the said Tho. dyed of the plague xxiijᵒ die.

Anno d'ni 1605 Regis Jacobi tertio.

C. James Ledsom *als.* Willson a bastard xped xxvᵒ die.
C. Isabell West doughter of James West of Hillom xped xxixᵒ die.

April.

B. Bridget Clark doughter of Thomas Clark above said dyed of the plague xvjᵒ
die. And heare the plagu ceased.
M. Thomas Allen and Alice Willson married xvijᵒ die. ·

May.

B. Will'm Sharp son of John Sharp of Hillom buried xxvijᵒ die.

June.

M. John Morley & Margaret Shan married xjᵒ die.
C.B. Alice Bond daughter of Gregory Bond of frieston xped and a male childe son
of the said Gregory Bond not christened died.
M. david Halalie and Idethe Smythies maried xvjᵒ die.
C. Mathew Lumby son of Mathew Lumby of frieston xped xxiijᵒ die.
C. Henry Leathom son of Thomas Leathom of frieston xped xxiiijᵒ.

Julie.

B. Alice Bond above said buried vᵒ die.
C. James Spinck son of John Spinck of Hillom xped xxvᵒ die.
August vacat.

Richard Bowling.
John Middlewood.

September.

M. John Irish and An Brough maried xvo die.
C. Margaret Burland daughter of Wᵐ Burland of Burton xped xxixo die.
B. John Robinson of Hambleton buried eod die.
C. Thoms Browne son of Will'm Browne of frieston xped eodem die.

October.

M. Xpofer Rawe & Margret Wilson maried xxijᵐo die.

November.

M. Thomas Beaw and Hellen Scrivener maried vo die.
C. John Rawlinson son of Rob'rt Rawlinson of friston xped viijo die.
M. John Brackoen and An Hamshire maried xijᵐo die.
C. John Procter son of John Procter of frieston xped xvijᵐo die.

December.

B. John Procter above said buried ijo die.
C. Thomas Warde son of Will'm Warde of Hillom xped vo die.
C. Margr't Nelson daughter of Will'm Nelson freeholder xped viijo die.

Januarie.

B. Gregorie Bond of frieston buried vjo die.
   Marie ffeild doughter of Rob'rt ffeild of Hillom xped xxvjo die.

ffebruarie.

C. Elizabeth Wells daughter of Edward Wells of Hillom xped ixo die.
C. Thomas Clarck son of Thomᵃs Clark of frieston xped xvjo die.
B. Dorothie Hayforth wief of Thomas Hayforth of hillom buried xviijo die.

March.

C. Will'm Norman son of Mʳ Roger Norman xped xxiijo die.

Anno d'ni 1606 Regis Jacobi Quarto.

C. Isabell Hallalie daughter of David Hallalie xped xxxo die.

Aprill.

C. Barbara Rawe daughter of Xpofer Rawe xped vjo die.
C. Matthew Hill son of Thomas Hill of Hillom xped xxvijo die.

May.

B. Jenet Tasker wief of Thomas Tasker of frieston buried xiiijo die.

Richard Bowling.
John Middlewood.

C. John Morley son of John Morley of frieston xped xxixo die.

June.

M. Will'm Gilliam and Jenet Brighton maried jᵐo die.
M. John Burnsall and Margaret Norman doughter of Mʳ George Norman of Burton salmon maried xvijo die.
B. Margaret Morley daughter of John Morley aforesaid buried xxjᵐo die.
C. Thomas Sharp son of John Sharp of hillom xped xxiiijo die.

Julie.

C. Will'm Tutill son of Thomas Tutill of Burton xped vo die.
C. Eupham Baker doughter of Will'm Baker xped xxo die.

M. Thomas Tasker & An Turpin maried xxij⁰ die.
B. John Crosland son of Peter Crosland buried xxij⁰ die.
C. James Leaper son of Thomas Leaper of hillom xped xxvij⁰ die.
C. Ellen Barker doughter of George Barker of Burton xped.
C. Will'm Spinck son of John Spinck of hillom xped eod. die.

August.

B. Will'm Nelson Senior buried vj⁰ die.
C. Marie Harrison doughter of Gyles Harrison xped x⁰ die.
C. Rob'rt Wilkinson son of Will'm Wilkinson of friston xped eod. die.
B. M'gret Browne doughter of John Browne buried xiiij⁰ die.
M. Will'm Turpin and Jane Kighley married xxiiij⁰ die.
M. Thomas Hayforthe and Elizabeth Cripling married xxvj⁰ die.

September vacat.

October.

B. John Baker buried iij⁰ die.
C. Thomas Spincke son of Rob'rt Spinck xped viij⁰ die.
M. Ralph Dobson & Ellyn Parker maried xij⁰ die.
C. Edward Robinson son of Edward Robinson xped xxij⁰ die.

November.

C. Marie Cuningham doughter of Mʳ Brian Cuningham xped ij⁰ die.
C. Will'm Beaw son of Thomas Beaw junior xped ix⁰ die.
M. Dynnys Slillitson & An Lake maried eod. die.
B. Christopfer Snawesdayll s'vant to Mʳ Willson buried xiij⁰ die.
M. Will'm Dussan & Elizabethe Greaves maried xxix⁰ die.

December.

C. Mary Sale doughter of Will'm Sale xped xiiij⁰ die.

Richard Bowling
Nicholas wauld.
Elias Lumax.
Robert feild.
Wᵐ Shippen.

Januarie.

C. Thomas Tasker son of Thomas Tasker xped vj⁰ die.
B. Will'm Sayle of hillom buried xvij⁰ die.
C. Will'm Procter son of John Procter xped xxj⁰ die.
B. Jenet Battell buried eodem die.
C. Joseph Fletcher son of John Fletcher junior xped xxv⁰ die.

ffebruarie.

B. John Rawlinson son of Rob'rt Rawlinson buried v⁰ die.
C. Bridget Nelson doughter of Will'm Nelson freholder xped vj⁰ die.

March.

B. Will'm Cuningham gent., buried vj⁰ die.
C. Will'm Burland son of Will'm Burland xped xij⁰ die.
B. Leonard Cowper of frieston died (supposed of the plague) xvij⁰ die.

Anno d'ni 1607 Regis Jacobi Quinto.

B. Ellyn Baker widowe buried xxix⁰ die.
C. Margaret Northen doughter of Andrew Northen xped ultimo die.

Aprill.

B. Thomas Bew the elder buried iiij^{to} die.
B. Elizabeth Norman daughter of Mr George Norman buried iiij^o die.
C. Jane Taler daughter of Wyll'm Tayler of Burton xped vij^o die.

May.

C. Thomas son of Richard Browne of hillom xped j^o die.
B. Eupham Norman daughter of Mr George Norman buried xj^o.

June.

M. John Berree and Jenet Muse married ij^o die.
B. Edward Robinson son of Edward Robinson buried xxiiij^{to} die.
C. Alice Dobson Doughter of Rob'rt Dobson xped xxv^o die.

Julie.

M. James Levet and Ellyn Hill maried xiiij^o die.
M. Richard Hay and Elizabethe Hembroughe maried xix^o die.
B. Elizabethe Welles doughter of Edward Wells buried xxij^o die.

August.

M. Robert Sugden and Hellen Man maried ix^o die.
C. B. John Bewe son of Thomas Bewe xped xviij^o die and buried eod. die.

> Richard Bowling.
> Will'm Nelson.
> Will'm Turpin.
> Edward Robinson.
> John Sharp.
> Will'm Tayler.

September.

M. Rob'rt West and Hellen Bond maried j^{mo} die.
M. Edward Wilson and Margaret Tutill maried vij^o die.
C. Agnes ffeild doughter of Rob'rt ffeild xped xxiiij^o die.

October.

B. Henry Smythies buried xj^o die.
B. Agnes ffeild above said buried xij^o Die.
M. John Hemyngway and Elizabeth Woodhowse maried xiij^o die.
M. Thomas Crud and Grace Sayl maried xxiiij^o die.
C. Jane Hallalee daughter of David Hallalee xped xxx^{mo} die.

November.

M. Richard Andrew and Agnes Emson married vij^o die.
C. Christopher Wilson son of Mr Will'm Wilson junior xped xvij^o die.

December.

C. William Wauld son of Nicholas Wauld xped iij^o Die.
B. Jenet Pereson of Burton widow buried x^o die.

Januarie.

C. George Spincke son of John Spincke xped iij^o die.
C. Margaret Baker daughter of Will'm Baker xped x^o die.
C. Richard Dawson son of Mathew Dawson xped xxiiij^o die.

ffebruarie.

B. Margaret Nellson doughter of Will'm Nellson freholder buried vj^o die.
C. Elizabeth Clark daughter of Thomas Clark xped xij^o die.

8

C. Brian Selbee son of George Selbee xped xiiijº Die.
B. Thomas Browne son of Will'm Browne buried xvº die.
B. Brian Selbee abovesd. buried xviijº Die.

March.

C. John the bastard son of Will'm Leaf and Isabell Snawden xped vjº die.
C. Elizabeth West daughter of James West xped xiijº die.

Anno domini 1608 Regis Jacobi Sexto.

B. A childe being doughter of Will'm Gilliam of hillom newly borne was buried xxxº die.

Aprill.

B. Thomas Wheldrake buried xxº die.
C. Will'm Hill son of Thomas Hill xped xxiiijº die.

> Rich: Bowling.
> Will'm Nelson.
> Edward Robinson.

May.

C. Thomas Welles son of Edward Welles xped jmo Die.
C. Will'm Hemmyngway son of John Hemyngway xped ixº Die.
C. Will'm Brigge son of Rob'rt Brigge xped xvº die.
M. ffraunces Cuningham and Margaret Crabtree married xvijº die.
M. Henry Perkin and Jenet Cowper married xvijº die.
C. John Berree son of John Berree xped xxixº die.
C. Richard Hallelee son of Rob'rt Hallelee xped xxixº die.

June.

C. John Wilkinson son of Will'm Wilkinson xped xijº die.
C. John Oulred son of Thomas Oulred xped xixº die.
C. Jane dewhirst doughter of Isaac dewhirst xped xxiiijº Die.
C. John Robinson son of Edward Robinson xped xxvjº die.

Julie.

C. Henrie Warde son of Will'm Warde xped xxvijº die.

August.

M. James Mitchelson and Isabell Smythies married iijº die.
C. Thomas Simson son of Thomas Simson a stranger xped vjº die.
C. Marie Wells doughter of Will'm Wells xped eod. die.
B. Will'm Hemmyngway above said buried xvº die.

September.

C. Robert Bew son of Thomas Bew xped iiijto die.
B. Thomas Bolton of Burton buried vjº die.
C. Elizabeth Nelson doughter of Will'm Nelson freeholder xped xvijº die.

October.

C. Edward Clarkson son of Roger Clarkson xped ijº die.
M. Thomas Walker and Isabell Hawley married viijº die.
B. Katheren Ellysse wief of John Ellysse buried xxvº die.
B. Nicholas Crosland son of Peter Crosland buried xxixº die.

November.

C. Isabell Chambers doughter of Thomas Chambers xped xviijº die.
B. Thomas Hayfoorth of Hillome buried xxixº die.

december vacat.

Januarie.

C. Alice Crud daughter of Thomas Crud xpned j^{mo} die.
B. John Fletcher ye parish Clerk buried xj^{to} die.
B. A childe not xped daughter of Richard Brown a stranger buried eodem die.

Richard Bowling.
John Morlay.

C. ffraunces Cuningham daughter of fraunces Cuningham xped xvij^o die.
C. Richard Morley son of John Morley xped xxix^o die.

ffebruarie.

C. Thomas Harrison son of Robert Harrison of Hurst Courtney in Birkin parish xped in frieston Churche.
C. John Harrison son of Giles Harrison xped xj^o die.
C. Alice Spinck daughter of John Spinck xped xxiiij^{to} die.

March.

C. Jane Leathome doughter of Thomas Leathom xped v^o die.

anno d'ni 1609 : Regis Jacobi Septimo : etc.

C. An Sugden daughter of Rob'rt Sugden xped xxix^o die.
C. John Parkin son of Henry Parkin xped xxix^o die.

aprill.

B. Alice Crosland wief of Peter Crosland buried v^o die.
B. Marie Johnson wief of Arthure Johnson & a newe borne infant Doughter of the said Arthure buried xiiij^{to} Die.
B. Marie Fletcher widowe buried xviij^o die.
B. Thomas Leaper buried xxix^o die.

May.

C. Susan Rawlinson Doughter of Rob'rt Rawlinson xped ix^o die.

June.

M. Will'm Middleton & Jane Morley married xx^o die.

Julie.

C. Bridget Turpin daughter of Will'm Turpin xped xiiij^o die.
C. Priscilla Coningham daughter of Mr Bryan Coningham xped xvj^o die.
B. John Oldred son of Thomas Oldred buried xxv^o die.

august.

B. George Spincke son of John Spincke buried xiiij^{to} die.
C. Will'm Browne son of Richard Browne xped xvj^{to} die.
C. Richard Spinck son of Rob'rt Spinck xped xx^o die.

September.

B. Thomas Welles son of Edward Welles buried ij^o die.

Richard Bowling.
Thomas Muce.
Thomas Clarke.

B. A younge infant daughter of John Hemmyngway not xped buried ij^o.
B. Alice Spinck daughter of John Spinck buried vj^o die.
C. Mary Gilliam daughter of Wm Gilliam xped x^{mo} die.
C. Jane Tutill daughter of Thomas Tutill xped xvij^{mo} die.
B. Katherine Cartwright widow buried xxvj^o die.

October.

C. John Dobson son of Rob'rt Dobson xped viij° die.
B. Jane Selbee wief of George Selbee buried ix° die.
C. Sibella Selbee doughter of the said George Selbee xped xj^{mo} die.
B. Thomas Nellson of Burton buried xxij° die.
B. An Hill doughter of Thomas Hill buried xxv° die.
C. Edward Sharp son of John Sharp xped xxviij° die.

november.

B. Robert Wilson son of Mr Will'm Wilson junior buried x^{mo} die.
B. Mary Wilson doughter of the saide Mr Wm Wilson buried xix^{no} die.
B. Robert Spinck buried xxiiij^{to} die.
M. Edward Stringer and Julian Irishe married xxviij° die.

December.

C. Michaell Browne son of Will'm Browne xped vj^{to} die.
B. Jane Johnson widowe buried ix° die.
C. Elizabeth Procter doughter of John Procter xped xxv° die.

Januarie.

B. Will'm Beaw son of Thomas Beaw buried xiiij° die.
M. John Dawson and Alice Middlewood married xxviij° die.

ffebruarie.

M. George Selbee & Margerie davie [or david] married iij^{tio} die.
M. Wm Cawpland & Elizabethe Willson married eodem die.
B. George Wray buried eodem iij^{tio} die.
B. Will'm Browne son of Richard Brown buried iiij^{to} die.
B. A yong infant not xped son of John fletcher buried v^{to} die.
B. John Wood buried xij^{mo} die.
B. Thomas Nettleton buried eodem die.
B. Isabell Ustler widow buried xv^{to} die.
B. An Lumax daughter of Elias Lumax buried xx^{mo} die.
B. Bridget Nelson daughter of Wm Nelson junior buried xxiiij^{to} die.
B. John Hutchinson buried eodem die.

Rich: Bowling.
Thomas Muce.
Thomas Clark.

March.

B. Rob'rt Wilkinson son of Will'm Wilkinson buried v^{to} die.
B. Margaret Wilkinson Doughter of Thomas Wilkinson of Adingham buried xxj^{mo} die.

Anno d'ni 1610 Regis. Jacobi octavo. &c.

C. Rob'rt Wilkinson son of Will'm Wilkinson xped xxv° die.
B. Henry Samson son of Rob'rt Samson buried ultimo die.

Aprill.

B. John Turpin buried xx^{mo} die.
C. Will'm Samson son of Robert Samson xped xxij° die.
C. Elizabeth Parkin doughter of Henry Parkin xped xxij° die.

May.

C. Elizabethe Cawpland doughter of Wm Cawpland xped xvij°.

June.

C. Edward Clark son of Thomas Clark xped primo die.
B. William Procter son of John Procter buried viij^{vo} die.
M. Robert Jeffreyson and Elizabeth Norman married xij^{mo} die.
B. Robert Cowper of Burton buried xv^{to} die.
M. Robert Craven and ffraunces Wray married xxiiij^{to} die.

Julie.

B. Isabell Chambers doughter of Thomas Chambers buried viij^{o} die.

august.

B. Mathew Lumbee son of Mathewe Lumbee buried vj^{to} die.
B. Alice Pereson widow buried ix^{no} die.
B. William Samson son of Robert Samson buried xiiij^{to} die.
C. Jane Dawson daughter of Mathewe Dawson xped xxvj^{to} die.

September.

C. John Howdell son of John Howdell of Burton xped xxiij^{tio} die.

October.

C. Margaret Dewhurste doughter of Isaac Dewhurst xped xij^{mo} die.

november.

B. Brian Turner and Agnes Pigburne married xj^{mo} die.

Richard Bowling.
Rob'rt Samson.
John Leathome.

M. Rob'rt Hamond & Jenet Warden maried xviij^{o} die.
B. James Wilbarne buried xviij^{o} die.
M. John Munckton and Elizabethe Ricroft maried xxv^{to} die.
M. Peter Crosland & Grace Dawson maried xxvj^{mo} die.
C. Will'm Berree son of John Berree xped xxx^{mo} die.

December vacat.

Januarie.

C. Robert Hemmyngway son of John Hemmyngway xped xxij^{o} die.

ffebruarie.

C. Elizabeth Tasker doughter of Thomas Tasker xped viij^{o} die.
C. Thomas Muce son of John Muce xped x^{mo} die.
C. Peter Browne son of Richard Browne xped xxviij^{vo} die.

March.

C. Robert West son of James West xped iij^{tio} die.
C. John the bastard son of Isabell Johnson xped iij^{tio} die.
C. Robert Harrison son of Giles Harrison xped xvij^{mo} die.

An'o d'ni 1611. Regis Jacobi nono &c.

C. Thomas Chambers son of Thomas Chambers xped xxvj^{to} die.

Aprill.

C. Elizabeth Sugden daughter of Rob'rt Sugden xped 14 die.
C. Margaret Wauld daughter of Nicolas Wauld xped xvij^{o} die.

may.

C. An Nelson doughter of Will'm Nelson freholder xped ij^{do} die.
B. John Pereson of frieston buried iiij^{to} die.

B. Beatrix Berree wief of Thomas Berree buried xviijᵒ die.
M. Peter Hemmyngway and Elizabeth Spinck maried xxviijᵒ die.

June.

C. James Wilbarne son of Nicholas Wilbarne xped xijᵐᵒ die.
C. Mark Rawlinson son of Rob'rt Rawlinson xped xvjᵗᵒ die.
B. Ellen Wilkinson wiefe of Will'm Wilkinson buried xxixⁿᵒ die.

Julie.

C. Robert Ward son of William Ward xped ijᵒ die.
C. Elizabeth Watson daughter of Brian Watson xped xxjᵒ die.
C. William Fletcher son of John ffletcher xped xxvᵒ die.

August.

B. Elizabethe Parkin daughter of Henrie Parkin buried vijᵐᵒ die.

> Richard Bowling.
> Will'm Swift.
> Will'm Nelson.
> John Bew.

B. Edward Rainer of South milfoord buried ixⁿᵒ die.
C. Laurence Craven son of Rob'rt Craven xped xjᵐᵒ die.
B. An Cowpe daughter of George Cowpe buried xxvᵗᵒ die.
B. Lawrence Craven son of the above named Rob'rt Craven buried xxxᵐᵒ die.

September.

C. John Baule son of Will'm Baule xped jᵐᵒ die.
C. Hellen Crud daughter of Thomas Crud xped vjᵗᵒ die.
C. Agnes Beaw daughter of Thomas Beaw xped viiijᵒ die.
B. Jenet Gilliam wief of Will'm Gilliam buried xjᵒ die.
C. Jane Feild daughter of Robert ffeild of Hillom xped xxiiijᵗᵒ die.
C. Jenet Hallalee daughter of Ellyfse Hallalee of South milford xped xxixᵒ die.

October.

B. Robert Wilkinson son of Will'm Wilkinson buried iiijᵗᵒ die.

november.

C. Frances Wilson son of Mʳ Wᵐ Wilson junior xped xvijᵒ die.

> December vacat.

Januarie.

C. An Robinson daughter of Edward Robinson xped vᵗᵒ die.
M. Thomas Elam and Susan Pereson married xxj die.
C. Grace Lavarock daughter of John Lavarock xped eodm 21ᵐᵒ die.
C. Alice Burland daughter of Will'm Burland xped xxixᵒ die.

ffebruarie.

C. Robert Stonas son of Leonerd Stonas xped ixⁿᵒ die.
C. William Cunningham son of Brian Cunningham gent. xped xxvijᵐᵒ die.
C. John Welles son of Edward Welles xped xxviijᵒ die.

march.

B. Grace Lavarock abouesaid buried vjᵗᵒ die.

Anno d'ni 1612. Regis Jacobi decemo &c.

C. William Hemmingway son of Peter Hemmingway xped xxvᵗᵒ die.
B. Thomas Nutter buried xxxjᵒ die.

Aprill.

B. Marie Crud wydow buried xixº die.
B. Margaret wief of Elias Lumax buried eodm die.

may.

B. ·Thomas Wensley buried xxiijº die.
C. frances Turpin doughter of Will'm Turpin xped xxiiijº die.

> Ri : Bowling.
> Nicolas Wauld.
> Wᵐ Baule.

June.

M. John Metcalf and Marie Elam married xxxº die.

Julie.

C. Margaret dawson doughter of Henrie dawson of Lumbe xped xixº die.
C. Marget Samson doughter of Rob'rt Samson xped xxixº die.

august.

C. Jane Hemmyngway doughter of John Hemmyngway xped xvº die.
C. John Hubee son of James Hubee xped xvjᵗº die.
B. William Wilkinson buried xxvijᵗʰ die.

September.

B. Suzan Elam wief of Thomas Elam buried vjᵗº die.
C. Thomas Leathom son of Thomas Leathom xped xxvijᵐº die.

October.

C. Jane Hamond doughter of Robert Hamond xped jᵐº die.
C. Charles Tutill son of Thomas Tutill xped xxᵐº die.
B. Mʳ Will'm Bew one of the Prebendaries of the collegiate churche of St. Wilfrid in Ripon buried xxvᵗº die.

november

M. Gregorie Middleton and Alice Leaper maried xº die.
M. John Barmingham and Alice Wray married xxijº die.
M. Robert Bocock and Margaret Guilliam married xxvjᵗº die.
M. Thomas Kinge and Elizabeth Leaper married xxviijº die.

December.

B. Roger Tailor buried ultimo die.

Januarie.

C. Elizabeth Craven doughter of Rob'rt Craven xped xvº die.
C. Thomas Feild son of Rob'rt ffeild xped xixº die.

ffebruarie.

M. Thomas Williman and Ann Benbow married ixº die.
C. Edward Procter son of John Procter xped xijº die.

march.

C. Elizabeth Berree doughter of John Berree xped iijº die.
C. Matthewe the basterd son of Ralph Preston and Beatrix Lawrence xped eodem die.

> Richard Bowling.
> Nicolas Wauld.
> Wᵐ Baule.

C. Faithe Nelson daughter of Will'm Nelson junior xped ix⁰ die.

anno d'ni : 1613 : regis Jacobi 11.

C. Richard Parkin son of Henrie Parkin xped xxv⁽ᵗᵒ⁾ die.

aprill.

B. Matthew Bramham buried xxv⁽ᵗᵒ⁾ die.
C. John Drabble son of Rob'rt Drabble xped eodem xxv⁽ᵗᵒ⁾ die.
B. John Middlewood buried xxviij⁰ Die.
B. Richard Norton buried xxx⁰ die.

may.

M. John Robinson and Jenet Bennetland married xxv⁽ᵗᵒ⁾ die.

June.

C. Jane dewhurst doughter of Isaac dewhurst xped xxvij⁰ die.
M. Wᵐ Hodson and Amee (?) Cartwryght married xxix⁰ die.
Julius vacat.
Augustus vacat.

September.

C. William Bocock son of Robert Bococke xped xix⁰ die.

October.

C. An Bermingham doughter of John Bermingham xped iij⁽ᵗᵒ⁾ die.
C. dorithie dawson Doughter of Matthew dawson xped v⁽ᵗᵒ⁾ die.
B. Jane dawson doughter of the said Mathew dawson buried x⁽ᵐᵒ⁾ die.
C. Isaac Williman son of Thomas Williman xped xviij⁰ die.
B. Isaac Williman abovesaid buried xxj⁽ⁱᵐᵒ⁾ die.
B. Phillip Halliley son of Elias Halliley whoe was slayne by a fall foorth of the bell chamber buried xxij⁰ die.
B. An Williman wief of the said Thomas Williman buried xxiij⁰ die.
C. Jane Browne daughter of Richard Browne xped xxiiij⁰ die.

november.

M. Richard Wilkinson and Agnes . . . . married vij⁽ᵐᵒ⁾ die.

December.

B. An Gilliam buried j⁽ᵐᵒ⁾ die.
B. A Basterd the supposed daughter frances Healde by Mary ffletcher buried x⁰ die.
B. Isabell Clerk wief of John Clerk buried xx⁰ die.

Januarie.

B. John Ellysse being excommunicate buried at the Winde Milne xiiij⁽ᵐᵒ⁾ die.
B. The doughter of Mʳ Will'm Wilson junior being a new born infant buried xxv⁰ die.

ffebruarie.

C. Dorithie Webster doughter of Robert Webster xped vj⁽ᵗᵒ⁾ die.

march.

C. Will'm West son of James West xped vj⁰ die.
B. Elizabeth Sugden doughter of Robert Sugden buried xiij⁰ die.

aprill anno d'ni 1614 Regis Jacobi : 12.

Mᵈ. Mʳ Edmund Bunny Prœbendarie of the Prœbend of Wistowe gave unto the parishioners of Monckfrieston tenne formes to remaine continually in there parishe churche to make use of for theire ease when they shall need them. These formes are chiefly made for the chauncell to bee used at the communion.

C. Alice dobson daughter of Ralph Dobson xped iij⁰ die.
C. Eupham Crudde daughter of Thomas Crudd xped xvij⁰ die.

may.

C. Isabell Hemmyngway daughter of John Hemmingway xped x⁰ die.
B. Thomas ffeild son of Robert ffeild buried xxiiij⁰ die.
B. Isabell darley buried eodem die.
C. John Anderson son of John Anderson xped xxvij⁰ die.
C. Thomas Bew son of Thomas Bew xped xxix⁰ die.

June.

B. Marie Sharp wief of John Sharp buried xvij^mo die.

Julie.

B. Leonard Sharp son of John Sharp abovesaid buried xxj^mo die.

august.

B. William Richardson buried xvj^to die.

september.

C. Beatrice Wauld daughter of Nicolas Wauld xped xiij⁰ die.
C. Ellen Hallaley daughter of David Hallaley xped xv⁰ die.

October.

B. Anne Spiser buried xx⁰ die.
C. Richard Harrison son of Giles Harrison xped xxiiij^to die.
B. dorothie dawson daughter of Matthew dawson buried xxviij⁰ die.

november.

B. Isabell Hamond wief of Will'm Hamond buried xxij⁰ die.
            December vacat.

Januarie.

C. Will'm Lee son of Thomas Lee xped ix⁰ die.
B. Margaret dowyn servant to James Woodrowe of Millfoorthe gent was perished in the snowe in Burton feilde as she came from Pomfret the xxj^th day and was buried xxij⁰ die.
C. Mary Procter daughter to John Procter xped xxix^no die.
M. Christopher Sherecroft and Alice Muse married xxxj^mo die.

ffebruarie.

C. Robert Tasker son of Thomas Tasker xped xvij⁰ die.
C. Jane Hemmyngway daughter of Peter Hemmyngway xped xxvj^to die.

march.

C. John Jackson son of Richard Jackson of Lumbe xped xij^mo die.
C. Alice Morret daughter of Thomas Morret of Milford xped xij^mo die.
C. Elizabeth Samson daughter of Rob'rt Samson xped xviij⁰ die.

anno d'ni 1615 : Regis Jacobi : 13.

B. M^res An Byrkby wife of Averey Byrkby Esquier buried xxix^mo die.

aprill.

B. Thomas Tasker buried ix⁰ die.
C. Thomas Hunter son of ffrances Hunter of South milfoord xped x^mo die.

9

C. Margaret Cawpland doughter of Jo: (?) Cawpland xped xvj^{to} die.
B. Mary Richardson wief of Hughe Richardson buried xviij^o die.
C. Jenet the basterd of ffrances ffairbarn and An Yeadon xped xxj^{mo} die.
C. Thomas Sugden son of Robert Sugden xped xxv^{to} die.
B. Jenet the basterd of ffrances ffairbarn buried xxix^{no} die.
C. John Turpin son of Will'm Turpin xped xxx^{mo} die.
   John Sharp of Hillom was drowned in his well and founde guilty of his owne
     death by the Jury and buried at Bettrice hil xvij^{mo} die Maii.
C. Hellen Craven doughter of Robert Craven xped xviij^o die.
C. Thomas Robinson son of Edward Robinson xped xxiij^o die.

June.

B. The son of John ffletcher newly borne buried iiij^{to} die.
B. Thomas Berree buried xiiij^{to} die.

Julie.

M. Will'm Ingle and Margaret Richardson married iiij^{to} die.

august.

C. Mary Nelson doughter of Will'm Nelson Junior xped j^{mo} die.
C. Rob'rt Emerson son of Rob'rt Emerson xped xviij^o die.

september.

B. An Beaw doughter of Thomas Beawe buried xvij^{mo} die.
                October vacat.

november.

C. Arthure Hamond son of Robert Hamond xped j^{mo} die.
B. Alice Sherecroft wife of xpofer Sherecroft of Lumbee buried iij^o die.
C. William Sherecroft son of the said xpofer Sherecroft xped eodem die.
C. Agnes dawson doughter of Henry dawson of Lumbee xped vij^{mo} die.
B. Jane Tutill wife of Thomas Tutill buried xvj^{to} die.
M. ffrances ffairbarne and An Yeaden married xxiij^o die.

December.

B. Mathew Lumbee buried xxij^o die.
C. Thomas Berre son of John Berre xped ultimo die.

Januarie.

B. Peter Hemmyngway buried xv^{to} die.
B. Margaret Cawpland doughter of William Cawpland buried xxiiij^{to} die.
M. ffrances Woode and Margaret Vevers marred xxvij^o die.

ffebruarie.

C. John Dillwoorth son of John Dillwoorth xped ij^o die.
C. Jenet Durnyll doughter of W^m durnyll xped xxj^o die.
B. John Dillwoorth above christned was buried ultimo die.

march.

B. Katherine Nettleton widow buried ij^o die.
B. Alice Allen wief of Thomas Allen buried v^{to} die.
C. Alice Backhouse *alias* Maunbee and Anne Backhouse *alias* Maunbe bastard
    children of Elizabeth Backhouse of South milfoord in Shereburn ꝑish and
    Richard Maunbe of Wistowe xped vj^{to} die.
B. Elizabeth Cawpland wief of Will'm Cawpland buried xvij^{mo} die.

anno d'ni 1616 : regis Jacobi 14.
aprill.
C.   Robert Ingle son of Will'm Ingle xped vij^{mo} die.

may.
B.   Hellen Talbot doughter of Antony Talbot of Heslewood buried xij^{mo} die.

June.
C.   Richard pearson son of John Pearson of Lumbee xped viij^o die.
C.   Jane ffletcher doughter of Will'm ffletcher of Milfoord xped xj^{mo} die.
C.   Elizabeth Hemmyngway doughter of Rob'rt Hemmyngway xped xxx^o die.

august.
B.   William Banester a woorkman at frieston hall buried xxiiij^{to} die.
B.   Grace Swift wife of Will'm Swift buried xxv^{to} die.
C.   Marie Crud doughter of Thomas Crud xped eodem die.
B.   William Swift above named buried xxviij^o die.

September.
B.   Thomas Tutill buried primo die.
C.   Margaret Bocock doughter of Rob'rt Bococke xped xxij^o die.

October.
C.   ffrances Webster doughter of Rob'rt Webster xped xx^o die.
M.   Thomas Diconson and Katherine Johnson married xxij^o die.
B.   Elizabeth Clarck wief of Thomas Clarck buried xxv^{to} die.
M.   Thomas Bowman & Isabel Boak married xxix^o die.
B.   ffrances Webster above named buried xxx^o die.

november.
M.   Alexander Norman and Mary Burland married v^{to} die.
B.   Will'm Ward buried xxix^o die.

december.
B.   Margery Fletcher wief of John ffletcher buried xxj^{mo} die.
B.   Jane Wilson doughter of Mr Will'm Wilson gent buried xxiij^o die.

Januarie.
C.   Margret Cawpland doughter of John Cawpland xped xxvj^o die.
C.   George the bastard son of George Hemmyngway and Ester Ingle (as she confesseth and averreth) xped eodem xxvj^o die.

ffebruarie.
B.   George the bastard of George Hemmyngway and Ester Ingle buried iij^o die.
C.   An Drable doughter of Rob'rt drable xped xvj^o die.
B.   John Walker buried xviij^o die.
C.   Alice Nelson doughter of Wm Nelson freholder xped xxviij^o die.

march.
B.   William Simson of Burton buried j^o die.
C.   Nepthali Bew son of Thomas Beawe xped ⎫ ix^o die.
C.   John Baly son of Brian Baly xped   ⎭
B.   Mary Crud doughter of Thomas Crud buried xxj^o die.

anno d'ni : 1617 : Regis Jacobi : 15.
aprill.
C.   John Hemmyngway son of John Hemmyngway xped xxij^o die.

B. Elizabeth Hemmyngway wief of John Hemmyngway buried xxvjᵒ die.
B. John Hemmyngway above xped buried xxvjᵒ die.

may.

B. Edward Welles buried ijᵈᵒ die.
C. George Barmingham son of John Barmingham xped iiijᵗᵒ die.
B. Isabell Mitchelson buried xᵒ die.

June.

M. Alexander Bramham and ffrances Walker married ijᵒ die.
B. James Hubee buried eodem die.
C. Elizabethe Sedall doughter of Vincent Sedall xped ixᵒ die.

Julie.

C. Thomas Lee son of Thomas Lee xped xiijᵒ die.

august.

B. Elizabeth Spinck doughter of John Spinck buried xᵒ die.
B. Isabell Bowman wief of Thomas Bowman buried xxvijᵐᵒ die.
C. Richard Grave son of Richard Grave xped xxvijᵐᵒ die.

september.

B. Jenet Durnyll doughter of Wᵐ Durnyll buried vjᵗᵒ die.
C. Mary ffairbarn doughter of ffrances ffairbarn xped xxjᵐᵒ die.
B. Alice Hunt widdow buried xxiijᵒ die.

October.

B. Isaac Dewehurst buried iiijᵗᵒ die.
B. Jenet Muse wief of Thomas Muse buried vᵗᵒ die.
M. Thomas Nutter and Margaret Hubee married vijᵐᵒ die.

november.

C.B. Wᵐ Hamond son of Rob'rt Hamond xped iiijᵗᵒ die buried vᵗᵒ die.
M. John Pearson & Alice Kighley James Bullock & Alice Rodes married vjᵗᵒ die.
M. George Tutell and Elizabethe Welles maried xiijᵒ die.
B. Margaret Watkin buried xvijᵐᵒ die.
M. Edmund Grant and Elizabethe Bramham married xviijᵐᵒ die.

december.

C. Rob'rt Procter son of John Procter xped xijᵐᵒ die.
                              Januarius vacat.

ffebruarie.

M. Gervase Barker and Margaret Lummax married iijᵒ die.
C. Rob'rt Procter son of John Procter buried xxjᵒ die.

march.

C. Robert Webster son of Robert Webster xped iiijᵗᵒ die.

anno d'ni : 1618 : Regis Jacobi : 16.

aprill.

C. Elizabeth Norman doughter of Alexander Norman xped xijᵐᵒ die.

may.

C. Elizabeth Bramham doughter of Alexander Bramham xped xᵒ die.
B. Katheren Turpin buried xiijᵒ die.
M. Thomas Clarke and Elizabeth Riddiall married xvjᵗᵒ die.

June.

C. Jenet Tutill daughter of George Tutill xped xj^{mo} die.
C. Hellen Craven daughter of Robert Craven xped xxvij^{o} die.

July.

B. Elizabeth Bramham above said buried x^{mo} die.
C. Katherine Anderson doughter of John Anderson xped xix^{o} die.
B. Guy Hallaly buried xxj^{mo} die.

august.

M. Thomas Bowman and Margaret Tomson married iiij^{to} die.
M. Will'm Grave and Elizabeth Hemmyngway married xj^{mo} die.
C. Jhon Pereson son of Jhon Pereson xped xxj^{mo} die.
C. Henry Emerson son of Rob'rt Emerson xped xxiij^{mo} die.

september.

B. Thomas Muse buried iij^{o} die Anno Ætatis 73°.
B. Margaret Cawpland doughter of John Cawpland buried ix^{o} die.
C. Grace Hemmyngway daughter of Robert Hemmyngway xped xx^{o} die
C. Elizabeth Wilson doughter of Mr Christofer Wilson xped xxj^{mo} die.

October.

C. John Nelson son of Will'm Nelson freeholder xped xvj^{to} die.
B. Mary Berree buried xxvij^{o} die.

november.

C. An Allen daughter of Thomas Allen xped j^{mo} die.
M. Cutbert Whiteley and Elizabeth draper married x^{mo} die.
C. Katharyn Barker daughter of Gervase Barker xped xxvij^{mo} die.
B. Thomas Watkin buried xxx^{mo} die.

december.

B. Katharine Barker above saide buried iij^{o} die.
C. Richard Shaw son of Will'm Shaw xped xiij^{o} die.
C. Mary dawson doughter of Henry dawson of Lumbee xped xx^{o} die.
B. Averey Byrkby Esquier buried xxviij^{o} die.
B. An durnyll doughter of W^{m} durnyll buried xxxj^{mo} die.

Januarie.

C. Margaret Shippen doughter of John Shippen of Milforth xped xv^{o} die.
M. John Lawnesdayle & Margery Grant married xxiiij^{to} die.
C. Susanna Norman doughter of Mr Will'm Norman xped xxvj^{to} die.

ffebruary.

M. Will'm Richardson & Katharine Nelson maried ij^{o} die.
C.B. Rob'rt Sugden son of Rob'rt Sugden xped and buried ix^{o} die.
C. Elizabeth Burland daughter of Wm Burland xped eodem die.
C. Will'm Grant son of Edmund Grant xped xxviij^{o} die.
B. Hellen Sugden wief of Robert Sugden buried eodem die.

march.

B. Richard Shawe son of Will'm Shaw buried xj^{mo} die.
C. William Procter son of John Procter xped xiiij^{to} die.
B. An Allen doughter of Thomas Allen buried xix^{o} die.

anno d'ni 1619 : regis Jacobi : 17.

C. William Robinson son of Edward Robinson xped xxxmo die.
B. Robert Rawlinson buried xxxjmo die.

April vacat.

may.

C. Mary Harrison doughter of Richard Harrison xped vjto die.
C. Thomas Roundell son of Thomas Roundell xped ixo die.
B. Thomas Roundell above said buried xxviijo die.

June.

C. John Richardson son of Will'm Richardson xped xvjto die.
M. Will'm Kitchen & Margaret dewhurst married xxvijo die.

July.

C. William Bramham son of Alexander Bramham xped xxijo die.

august.

C. An Lownsdayll doughter of John Lownsdayll xped viijo die.

september.

C. Alice Short doughter of John Short of Mylford xped jo die.

October.

C. Thomas Nutter son of Thomas Nutter xped xviij die.

november.

M. Will'm Nettleton & Margaret Welles married ixo die.
B. Christopher Wilson Gent buried xjo die.
C. Thomas durnyll son of Will'm durnyll xped xxviijo die.

Januarie.

C. Will'm Turpin son of Will'm Turpin xped jo die.
C. Will'm the Bastard of Mary Crosland xped xvjo die and buried xxxo die.

ffebruary.

M. Thomas Holmes & Alice Cook maried xviijo die.

anno d'ni 1620 : regis Jacobi : 18.
march.

C. Mary Bocock doughter of Robert Bocock xped ⎫
C. Mary Gylliam doughter of George Gilliam xped ⎬ xxvjo die.
C. Elizabeth Shaw doughter of Will'm Shaw xped xxviijo die.

aprill.

C. Matthew Lee son of Thomas Lee xped ijo die.
C. Jane dawson doughter of matthew dawson xped xxiijo die.
C. John Muse son of Nicolas Muse xped xxxo die.

may.

B. John Morley of South milford buried vto die.
C. John ffairbarn son of ffrances ffairbarn xped vijo die.
C. Isabell Roundell doughter of Thomas Roundell xped vijo die.
M. Antony Johnson and An Clough married ixo die.
B. An Arlyn buried xjo die.
C. James Hamond son of Robert Hamond xped xixo die.
C. Thomas Craven son of Robert Craven xped xxvto die.

June.

C. William Norman son of Will'm Norman gent xped v^{to} die.
C. Mary Hallalee daughter of Antony Hallalee of Lumbe xped vj^{to} die.
B. Isabell wyfe of Thomas Grant buried viij^{o} die.
B. Will'm Norman abovesaid buried xvij^{o} die.
C. Jane Berre daughter of John Berre xped ⎫ xxix^{o} die.
C. Elizabeth Pereson daughter of John Pereson xped ⎭

Julius vacat.

august.

M. John Hemmyngway & An Walker married xxix^{no} die.
C. Thomas son of Richard Avaray xped xxx^{o} die.

September.

C. John Walker son of George Walker xped x^{o} die.
B. Dorothy Watkyn widow buried xx^{o} die.

October.

C. Elizabeth fflynt doughter of Ralph flynt of mylforth xped.
M. Matthew Hube & Mary Berridge married xxiiij^{o} die.

november.

C. Elizabeth Grave doughter of Richard Grave xped v^{o} die.
M. Will'm Knowles & Mary Askam married eodem die.
C. Robert Richardson & Edward Richardson sons of Will'm Richardson xped ix^{o} die.
B. Edward Richardson abovesaid buried xviij^{o} die.
M. Thomas Smythe & Hellen Tomson married xix^{mo} die.
B. John ffyddlyn buried xxx^{mo} die.

december.

M. William Welles & Mary Rhodes married ix^{o} die.
B. Robert Richardson abovesaid buried x^{mo} die.
C. Jane Lowson doughter of Rob'rt Lowson xped xxxj^{mo} die.

Januarie.

C. Mary Norman daughter of Alexander Norman xped j^{o} die.
C. Margaret Pereson doughter of John pereson of Lumbee xped vij^{o} die.
B. Matthew Lee son of Thomas Lee buried viij^{o} die.
C. Thomas Tutell son of George Tutell xped xxiij^{o} die.

ffebruarie.

C. Robert Hemmyngway son of Robert Hemmyngway xped iiij^{to} die.
M. Roger Bew and Elizabeth Atkinson married vj^{to} die.
M. Will'm Cocker and Margaret Johnson married vij^{mo} die.
B. Arthure Hamond buried xiiij^{o} die Anno Œtatis 78.
C. Margaret ffeild doughter of Robert ffeild xped xv^{to} die.
M. John Atkyn and Hellen Marshall married xxij^{o} die.
C. Will'm Hallale son of Will'm Hallale xped xxij^{o} die.
B. Mary Hallale wife of the said Will'm Hallale buried xxv^{to} die.

march anno d'ni: 1621: Regis Jacobi: 19.

C. John Atkin son of John Atkyn xped xxviij^{to} die.
C. Mary Welles doughter of Will'm Wells xped xxxj^{o} die.

aprill.

C. George Norman son of Mr Will'm Norman xped xvj^{to} die.
B. George Lownsdayle son of John Lownsdayle xped xviij^{to} die.

B.   George Lownsdayle abovesaid buried xxij⁰ die.
B.   Margery Lownsdayle wief of John Lownsdayle buried xxiiij^to die.
C.   Richard, Howdell son of Henry Howdell xped xxvij⁰ die.

may.

B.   Mary Feild daughter of Robert ffeild buried xv⁰ die.
B.   Hellen Howdayle wief of Robert Howdell buried xxix⁰ die.

June.

B.   Katharyn Anderson doughter of John Anderson buried x^mo die.
C.   Will'm Cocker son of Wm Cocker xped xx⁰ die.
C.   Margaret drabble doughter of Robert drabble xped xxx⁰ die.

July.

C.   Mary Hubee doughter of Matthew Hubee xped xiij⁰ die.
M.   Richard North and Elizabeth Norton married xvij⁰ die.

august.

C.   Bridget Emerson daughter of Robert Emerson xped xiij⁰ die.
B.   Mr Thomas Norman buried xiiij⁰ die.
B.   Edward Ledsham buried xxij⁰ die.
B.   Margaret ffeild doughter of Robert ffeild buried xxvj^to die.

September.

M.   John Baynes & Mary Roundell married xxx⁰ die.

October.

C.   Frances Ledsam daughter of Elizabeth Ledsam wydow xped iij⁰ die.
C.   Richard Procter son of John Procter xped xiiij^to die.
B.   Frances Ledsam abovesaid buried xx⁰ die.

november.

C.   Joan Bramham doughter of Alexander Bramham xped xviij⁰ die.
M.   ffrances Watkin & Elizabeth dawson married xxv⁰ die.
B.   George Norman of Burton Esquier buried xxviij^to die.

december.

B.   Thomas Beaw buried xxiij⁰ die.

Januarie.

C.   Elizabeth Roundell doughter of Thomas Roundel xped xv⁰ die.

ffebruary.

B.   John Middlewood buried xvij⁰ die.

marche.

C.   George Bewe son of Roger Bewe xped j^no die.
C.   Elizabeth ffairbarne daughter of ffrances ffairbarne xped vij⁰ die.
B.   Margaret Shereburne buried x⁰ die.
C.   Frances Norman son of Mr Wm Norman xped xvij⁰ die.

anno d'ni 1622:   *Reg: Jacobi* 20.

C.   Isabell Muse doughter of Nicolas Muse xped xxxj die.

aprill.

C.   Alice Gilliam doughter of George Gilliam xped x⁰ die.
B.   Alice Gilliam above said buried xiij⁰ die.

may.

B. Elias Lummax buried iiij^{to} die.
C. Jane Barmingham doughter of John Barmingham xped xxiij° die.

June.

B. Sr Francis Baylden Knight buried xxiiij° die.
B. Mary daughter of George Gylliam buried eodem die.

July.

B. Wydowe Turner buried vj^{to} die.
M. John Jackson and Margaret Jackson married vij^{to} die.

august.

C. Bridget doughter of John Anderson xped xiiij^{to} die.
B. Mt^{res} An Colbye buryed xvij^{mo} die.

                                    Septemb^r et october vacant.

november.

C. John Harrison son of Richard Harrison xped j^{mo} die.
M. John Gylson and Jane Berredge marryed xij^{mo} die.
B. Isabell Yeaden widowe buried xxiij° die.

december.

M. Thomas Sayner and Hellen Bew married iij° die.
B. Robert Emerson son of Robert Emerson buried xx° die.
C. William Bramham son of George Bramham xped xxvj^{to} die.

Januarie.

C. Margaret Hubee doughter of Matthew Hubee xped j° die.
B. Mary the wief of Will'm Shippen buried eodem die.
C. Dorothy doughter of John Pereson of Lumbee xped v^{to} die.
B. Wydowe Wray buried vj^{to} die.
C. Frances Lowson son of Robert Lowson xped xiiij^{to} die.
C. Elizabethe Cocker doughter of Will'm Cocker xped xxix^{no} die.
B. Mary Baynes wief of John Baynes of Milforth buried xxxj^{mo} die.
C. Elizabethe Baynes doughter of the saide John Baynes xped eodem xxxj^{mo} die.

ffebruary.

M. William Leathome and An Norton married ij° die.
C. John Barker sonne of Gervase Barker xped eodem ij° die.
C. George Shaw son of William Shaw xped vj° die.
B. Jane Browne a poore widdow of Newcastle traveilling to the Barthes dyed here and was buried xv^{to} die.

march.

B. John Cook a vagrant begger dwelling as hee affirmed at Wauldbee dyed at Hillom and was buried xij° die.
B. Thomas Williamson servant to Wm Hollingwoorth buried xiij° die.

                anno d'ni : 1623 : regis Jacobi 21.

aprill.

B. John Walker a vagrant begger buried xj^{mo} die.
C. Tobias Blakiston son of Mr Marmaduke Blakiston xped xiiij° die.
C. John Norman son of Mr William Norman xped xv^{to} die.
M. George Bew and Alice Wilkinson married xxiij° die.

may.

B. Robert drable buried ij⁰ die.
B. Susanna Norman daughter of Mʳ Wᵐ Norman buried viij⁰ die.
B. Will'm Bell buried xviij⁰ die.
C. Jennet Roundell daughter of Thomas Roundell xped xviij⁰ die.
C. John Hollingwoorth son of Will'm Hollingwoorth xped xxvj⁰ die.

June.

C. Robert Hallale son of Antony Hallalee of Lumbee xped j⁰ die.
M. Antony Burland and Jenet Bramham married x⁰ die.
B. Jennet Roundel daughter of Thomas Roundell buried xix⁰ die.
C. Elizabeth Diconson daughter of Edmund Diconson of dranfeild in Darby shire a Cowper xped xxvj⁰ die.

July.

M. William Bayles & Alice Robinson marrried viij⁰ die.
B. Richard Dice was found drowned in a pit wᵗʰin frieston Ings & was buried xxx⁰ die.

august.

B. Hughe Richardson buried iij⁰ die.
C. Elizabeth Hamond daughter of Robert Hamond xped xxvij⁰ die.
C. John Bew son of George Bew xped xxx⁰ die.

September.

C. George Welles son of George Welles xped xvij⁰ die.

October.

M. William Heptenstall & Mary Waude married xiiij⁰ die.

november.

C. Elizabeth Wauld daughter of Nicolas Wauld xped ij⁰ die.
C. Bridget Bocock daughter of Robert Bocock xped eod ij⁰ die.
C. Jane Gylson daughter of John Gylson of Burton xped ix⁰ die.
C. Henry Leathom son of William Leathom xped eodem ix⁰ die.
C. Marmaduke Gilliam son of George Gilliam xped xj⁰ die.
B. Jane Bristow a Vagrant beggar buried xxviij⁰ die.
C. Will'm Tod son of John Tod xped xxviij⁰ die.

december.

C. Elizabeth Tutill daughter of George Tutill xped x⁰ die.
C. Vincent Pearson son of John Pearson xped xj⁰ die.
M. Cuthbert Bramham & Isabell ffreeman married xiij⁰ die.
B. Richard Andrewe buried xxx⁰ die.

Januarie.

B. Isabell Norton Wydowe buried xxiij⁰ die.
C. Isabell Nelson daughter of Will'm Nelson freeholder xped xxix⁰ die.

ffebruary.

B. An Birredge wyddowe buried iiij⁰ die.

march.

B. Jennet Bellabee wief of Wᵐ Bellabee buried v⁰ die.

anno d'ni 1624 : reg : Jacob : 22 :

aprill.

John Bewe son of George Bewe buried ijᵒ die.
Elizabethe doughter of Thomas Allen buried ixᵒ die.
Robert Webster buried xjᵒ die.
Bettrice Blakiston doughter of Mʳ Marmaduke Blakiston xped xviijᵒ die.
Bridget Richardson doughter of Wᵐ Richardson xped xxvijᵒ die.
Robert Walker & Bridget Middlewood married xiijᵒ die.

may.

Rosamund Chatterton doughter of Mʳ Edmund Chatterton xped xxvᵗᵒ die.

June.

Mary Welles doughter of William Welles buried xvjᵗᵒ die.

July.

Isabell Nellson doughter of Will'm Nelson freeholder buried iijᵒ die.
Jane Roundell doughter of Thomas Roundell xped xiijᵒ die.
Hellen Avara doughter of Richard Avara xped xviijᵒ die.
Elizabeth ffawcett buried xxiiijᵗᵒ Die.
James Webster son of Widow Webster xped xxvᵗᵒ die.
Elizabeth Hamond doughter of Robert Hamond buried xxviijᵒ die.
                    Augustus vacat.

september.

George Rogers & Jenet Oldred married vᵗᵒ die.
Mʳ Mathew Kay & Mʳˢ Elizabeth Wilson married vijᵒ die.
Thomas Bew son of Roger Bew xped xjᵒ die.
Thomas Muse son of Nicolas Muse xped xiiijᵗᵒ die.
Mary Norman wife of Alexander Norman buried xvijᵒ die.
                    October vacat.

november.

Jane doughter of Robert Hemyngway xped xiiijᵒ die.
dorothy wief of Henry Inglot buried xvᵒ die.
Tobias Blakiston son of Mʳ Marmaduke Blakiston buried xxjᵒ die.
Leonerd Bustard & Elizabeth Haram married eod die.
Jane Bramham doughter of George Bramham xped eod die.
Will'm Arnold son of Will'm Arnold xped xxiiijᵒ die.
Margaret Feild wief of Mʳ Robert ffeild buried xxviijᵒ die.

december.

John Harrison son of Richard Harrison buried xjᵒ die.
dorothie Walker wife of Geore Walker buried xiiijᵒ die.
Waryn Walker son of George Walker xped eod die.
Garvase Norman son of Mʳ Will'm Norman xped xixᵒ die.

Januarie.

Richard Shippen son of John Shippen of Milfoorth xped ixᵒ die.
Christopher Cocker son of Wᵐ Cocker xped xvjᵒ die.
Lancelott Bew son of George Bew xped xxᵒ die.
An Nelson doughter of Wᵐ Nelson freeholder buried xxijᵒ die.
Thomas Bramham son of Cutbert Bramham xped xxiijᵒ die.

ffebruarie.

B. Mary Nelson doughter of Wm Nelson freholder buried iij^o die.
M. Thomas ffoyster & Margaret Wray married vij^o die.
M. George Spink & Dorothy Wauld married viij^o die.

march.

C. Stephen Westerman son of Joseph Westerman xped } xiij^o die.
C. Will'm Emerson son of Robert Emerson xped
C. Robert Wells son of George Welles xped xvj^o die.
C. Frances Ledsam doughter of John Ledsam xped xx^o die.

anno d'ni 1625: reg: Jacob: 23.

B. Jenet Drable widow buried xxv^{to} die.

anno reg: Caroli: primo.

aprill.

C. Margaret ffairbarn doughter of ffrances ffairbarn xped iij^o die.
B. M^{res} Margaret Wilson Widow buried iiij^{to} die.
B. ffrances ffairbarn buried vj^{to} die.
C. Edward Walker son of Robert Walker xped vij^o die.
B. Garvase Norman son of Mr Will'm Norman buried xix^o die.
B. Elizabeth Lumbee widdow buried xxj^o die.
C. Thomas procter son of John procter xped xxj^o die.
C. Elizabeth doughter of Henry Howdell of South Milforth xped xxix^o die.

Maius vacat.

June.

C. Mary Blakiston doughter of Mr Marmaduke Blakiston xped xix^o die.
M. Michael Pearson & An Symson married xxix die.

July.

C. Elizabeth Hemmyngway doughter of George Hemyngway xped x^o die.

august.

C. Richard Walwark son of James Walwark of Oldam in Lancshire xped xxviij^o die.

September.

C. Will'm Hurtley son of John Hurtley of Lennarton xped xxv^{to} die.
C. Elizabeth Gylson doughter of John Gylson xped xxx^o die.

October.

C. An Hallalee doughter of Antony Hallalee of Lumbee xped ij^o die.
C. ffrances Grave doughter of Richard Grave xped ix^o die.
M. John Browne & Alice Grave married xj^{mo} die.
C. Will'm Geldar son of Will'm Geldar xped xiij^o die.
M. Henry Blakiston Gent & Mary Stubbes married xxiij^o die.

november.

B. Will'm Geldar abovesaid buried j^o die.
M. Will'm Harrison & Bridget Gilliam married vij^o die.
C. Martyn Hickinbottom son of Will'm Hickinbottom xped xiij^o die.
M. Henry Inglot & Margret Bramham married xv^{to} die.
C. Will'm Leathom son of Will'm Leathom xped xx^o die.
C. Jane Norman doughter of Mr Will'm Norman xped xxij^o die.
M. Thomas Green & Margaret Anderson married xxviij^o die.

december.

C. Nicolas Quantforth son of Rob't Quantforth of North Cowton a stranger xped xj⁰ die.
C. Elizabeth Gilliam doughter of George Gilliam xped xviij⁰ die.

Januarie.

M. Mr Vincent Siddall & M^res Margaret Pickering married ij⁰ die.
B. An Berree buried vj^to die.

ffebruarie.

B. Jenet Kay of Lumbee widdowe buried j⁰ die.
C. Mary Roundell doughter of Thomas Roundell xped xij⁰ die.
C. George Kellingley son of Will'm Kellingley xped xxj^mo die.

march.

C. Isabell the basterd of An Tottee and John Dillmorth (? Dillworth) as shee the said An confessethe xped xj⁰ die.

anno d'ni 1626: regis Caroli: 2:

C. B. W^m son of John Anderson xped xxviij⁰ die buried xxx⁰ die.

aprill.

B. An ffairbarne doughter of widow ffairbarne buried x⁰ die.
B. A vagrant boy about the age of twelve yeares buried eodem die.
C. Martha Barmingham doughter of John Barmingham xped xxv^to die.

may.

C. Marget Shaw doughter of Will'm Shaw xped xviij⁰ die.

June.

M. George Colly and Jenet Sale married xj⁰ die.
C. John Hemmyngway son of Richard Hemmyngway xped xiij⁰ die.

July.

C. Katharine doughter of Richard Morton of Lumbee xped ij⁰ die.
M. Richard Wilkinson & Elizabeth Robinson married iiij^to die.
C. Marget Bywater doughter of Thomas Bywater xped xxx⁰ die.

august.

B. Will'm Tailer of Burton buried j^mo die Anno Œtatis 93.
C. Isabell Harrison doughter of Richard Harrison xped vj^to die.
M. Mr Launcelot Hall minister of this church & Katherine Richardson married xv^to die.
B. Roger Bew buried xxvj^to die.

september.

C. Robert Birredge son of Robert Birredge xped vj^to die.
C. Jane Tod doughter of John Tod xped x⁰ die.
C. B. Jane Tutill doughter of George Tutill xped & an Infant buried xvj^to die.
C. Robert Pereson son of Michael Pereson xped at Brotherton xxv^to die.

October.

B. Joan Bew widdow buried ij die vixit annos 66 mensem j Hebd duas.
M. Wm Bellabe & An Andrew married iij⁰ die.
B. Marget ffoister wief of Thomas ffoyster buried iiij^to die.
C. Jennet ffoister doughter of ye saide Thomas ffoister xped eodem die.

B. Elizabeth Wilson doughter of Christofer Wilson late of Monckfrieston gent deceased buried xvij⁰ die.
B. An Allen wife of Thomas Allen buried xxxj⁰ die.

november.

B. Jennet ffoister doughter of Thomas ffoister buried j^mo die.
C. Elizabeth Walker daughter of Robert Walker xped ⎫ v^to die.
C. Elizabeth Collier doughter of George Collier xped ⎭
M. James Roundell & Elizabeth Willson married ⎫ ix⁰ die.
M. James Clay & Mary Samton married ⎭
B. Peter Bowes buried x⁰ die.
M. Henry Green & ffrances Howdell married ⎫ xiijmo die
B. Elizabeth Tailer widdowe buried ⎭
M. George Wauld & Jane Muse married xxj⁰ die.
B. Thomas Letham buried xxij die.
B. Robert Emerson buried ⎫ xxv^to die.
B. Thomas West buried ⎭
M. Edward Lund & Mary Sale married xxvij⁰ die.
C. Edmond Hemmyngway sonne of George Hemmyngway xped xxx⁰ die.

december.

C. John Spinck son of Thomas Spinck xped vij⁰ die.
C. Jane Inglot daughter of Henry Inglot xped xxvj^to die.
B. William Hamond buried xxvij⁰ die vixit annos 77 : mens 9 : dies 2.
C. Thomas Blakiston son of Mr Marmaduke Blakiston xped xxxj⁰ die.

Januarius vacat.

ffebruarie.

B. John Spinck yeoman buried primo die Anno Œtatis 68.
B. Martha doughter of John Barmingham buried xiiij⁰ die.
B. Will'm Bell buried xvj^to die.
B. Alexander Bramham buried xxj⁰ die.
C. Mary doughter of Will'm Cocker xped xxiij⁰ die.
B. Will'm Holdswoorth buried xxviij⁰ die.

march.

C. Mary Ledsam doughter of John Ledsam xped xj⁰ die.
C. Mary Norman doughter of Mr Wm Norman xped xiij⁰ die.
B. Tymothy Bramham buried eodem die.

anno domi : 1627 : reg : Caroli : 3 :

aprill vacat

may.

C. John Bew son of George Bew xped j^mo die.
C. Robert Hall son of Mr Lancelot Hall xped xiiij^to die.
M. Robert Turner and Jane Tailer married xxj⁰ die.

June.

C. Marmaduke Harbut son of George Harbut xped vij^mo die.

July.

B. Isabel Rud wief of Edmund Rud buried j^mo die.
B. Jane Bywater wief of Thomas Bywater buried ij⁰ die.
C. Elizabeth Spinck daughter of George Spinck xped viij⁰ die.
C. Jane Muse doughter of Nicolas Muse xped xv^to die.

august.

M. John Anderson & ffrances Bramham married vj^to die.
C. Richard Roundell son of James Roundell xped xxvj^to die.

September.

M. John Lownsdaile & Agnes Crosland married ix^o die.

October.

C. Hellen Green doughter of Henry Green xped xij^o die.
B. Will'm Hay of Lumbee buried xxvj^to die.
C. William Gylson son of John Gylson xped xxviij^o die.

november.

M. Mr Thomas Gearrerd & M^res Margaret Ellysse married vj^to die.
B. Isabell Huscroft buried xix^o die.
C. Thomas Hallalee son of Antony Hallalee of Lumbee xped xxv^to die.

december.

C. Tomisen Roundell daughter of Thomas Roundell xped xvj^to die.
B. Jennet Baxter widow buried eodem die.
C.B. Elizabeth Bustard daughter of Leonard Bustard xped xxiij^o die & buried xxix^o
     die.

Januarie.

B. John Anderson buried vj^to die.
B. ffrances Craven wief of Robert Craven buried x^mo die.
B. Isabel Snawesden buried eodem die.
B. Will'm Nelson freeholder buried xxv^to die.

ffebruarie.

C. Richard Gilliam son of George Gilliam xped tertio die.
B. Bridget Emerson daughter of Widowe Emerson buried xix^o die.
B. Robert Bocock buried xxiij^o die.
C. Bartholomew Bramham son of George Bramham xped xxiiij^o die.

march.

C. Jennet Turner daugter of Robert Turner xped xix^o die.
C. James the bastard son of dority Bustard and Mr Thomas Estoft (as upon her
     examination by the grace wief in her travell she confessed and solemly pro-
     tested) xped xxv^o die 1628.

anno d'ni : 1628 : reg : Carol : 4.

aprill.

B. Bridget Bocock dawhter of Marget Bocock buried xxj^mo die.
B. dorothy Walker daughter of Robert Walker buried xxiij^o dīe.

may.

C. Jane Hemmyngway daughter of George Hemyngway xped xiiij^o die.
C. Christofer son of John Barmingham xped xviij^o die.
B. Elizabeth daughter of Nicolas Waud buried eodem die.
B. John Leaf buried xx^o die.

June.

B. Alice Tomson daughter of ffrancis Tomson of Brotherton buried xx^o die.
C. Will'm Collier son of George Collier xped xxij^o die.
C. Mary dawson daughter of John Dawson of Lumbe xped xxix^mo die.

Julie.

C. Susan Welles daughter of George Welles xped iijo die.
B. Thomas Blakiston son of Mr Marmaduke Blakiston buried vijo die.
M. Mr Thomas Wood & Susan Piggot married xjmo die.

August.

B. James Inglot buried iijo die.
C. An daughter of Robert Hemyngway xped eodem die.
C. Elizabeth Hube Daughter of Matthew Hubee xped xxiiijo die.

September.

M. Mr Thomas Blakiston & Mres Hellenor Addisall married ijo die.
C. Thomas Spinck son of Thomas Spinck xped xxjmo die.
                                        October vacat.

november.

C. Hellen Tutill daughter of Alexander Tutill xped jmo die.
C. John Walker son of Robert Walker xped xmo die.
M. John Harrison and An Hickinbottom married xjmo die.
M. John Earbee and Margaret Hemyngway married xijmo die.
C. George Wauld son of George Wauld xped xixno die.
M. Will'm Clean & Jane Rocliff married xxmo die.
M. Will'm Barber & Elizabeth Lumbe married xxvijmo die.

december.

M. Robert Burnyll & Mary Chester married xvjo die.
C. Isabel Leatham daughter of Will'm Leatham xped xxvijo die.

Januarie.

B. John Walker abovesaid buried iijtlo die.
C. Thomas Pereson son of John Pereson xped xvto die.
C. An Lund daughter of Edward Lund xped xviijo die.

ffebruarie.

C. Thomas Norman son of Mr Will'm Norman xped viijo die.
M. Will'm Robert and Elizabeth Clark married xjmo die.
B. Matthew Collier buried xijmo die.
B. Edmund Rud buried xxvijo die.
B. Widow Inglot buried xxviijo die.

march.

B. Thomas Oldred buried iiijto die.
C. Will'm Hemyngway son of Richard Hemyngway xped xxijo die.

anno d'ni : 1629 : reg : Car. 5to.

aprill.

C. George Dawson son of Randall Dawson xped xijo die.
C. John Bustard son of Leonard Bustard xped xixno die.
C. Susan Shaw daughter of Will'm Shaw xped xxiijo die.
                                        Maius vacat.

June.

B. Alexander Norman buried viijo die.
M. Robert Craven & Elizabeth Bustard married xiiijto die.
M. George ffoister & Elizabeth Green married xvjto die.
B. A new born Infant son of William Clean buried xxjmo die.

July.

Thomas ffoister & Margaret Wells married xiiij° die.
Richard Harrison son of John Harrison xped xxvj^to die.

august.

Arthure Cocker son of Will'm Cocker xped ix° die.
Henry Roundell & Elizabeth Middlewood married xviij° die.

September.

Margaret Blakiston daughter of Mr Marmaduke Blakiston xped xiij° die.
An Pearson daughter of Michael Pearson xped xx° die.

October.

Widow Andrew buried iiij^to die.
Elizabeth West daughter of James West buried eodem die.
John Turner son of Robert Turner xped xviij° die.
Isabell Barber daughter of Wm Barber xped eodem die.
Vincent Siddall & Mary Johnson married xxvj° die.
George Spincke son of George Spinck xped xxviij° die.

november.

James West buried xv^to die.
An Ledsam daughter of John Ledsam xped } xxij° die.
ffrancis Roundell daughter of Thomas Roundell xped }
George Lumax & Elizabeth Roydhouse married xxviij° die.
Matthew Hollingwoorth & Jane Hemyngway married xxix° die.

december.

Will'm Walker son of Robert Walker xped xij^mo die.

Januarie.

Thomas Chambers buried viij° die.
John Gylson son of John Gylson xped xvij° die.
Mary Illingwoorth daughter of John Illingwoorth xped xxxj^mo die.

ffebruarie.

William Roundell son of James Roundell xped xiiij° die.
Helinor Guilliam daughter of George Guilliam xped xvij^mo die.

march.

ffrances Muse son of Nicolas Muse xped x^mo die.
An Collier daughter of George Collier xped xiiij^mo die.

anno d'ni 1630: *regis Car:* 6to.

Thomas Muse son of Nicolas Muse buried xxvij° die.

aprill.

Peter Danyell a poore man buried vij^mo die.
ffrancis Eggrom buried xj^mo die.
Margaret Tod daughter of John Tod xped xviij^mo die.

may.

An ffoister daughter of Thomas ffoister xped xvij^mo die.
Joan Bew daughter of George Bew xped xxix die.

June.

B.   Dorothy daughter of Nicolas Hemyngway buried x^mo die.

                              Julius vacat.

august.

B.   A newborne Infant daughter of Margaret Mawdsley a vagrant woman buried xxviij^o die.

september.

B.   ffrancis dawson wief of Matthew dawson buried vj^to die.
B.   Jane Roundel daughter of Thomas Roundel buried xxvj^to die.

november.

C.   ffrancis Wauld son of George Wauld xped j^mo die.
B.   Richard Nelson & Elizabeth Leatham buried ij^o die.
B.   John Leatham buried xiiij^o die.
M.   Ralph Roberts and Margaret Smith married xvj^to die.
B.   Margaret Hollingwoorth buried xij^o die.
C.   Will'm & John Lund sons of Edward Lund xped xxiij^o die.
B.   Mary Lund wief of the sd. Ed. Lund buried eod. die.
B.   John Lund aforesaid buried xxviij^mo die.

december.

B.   Will'm son of Ed. Lund aforesaid buried iij^tio die.
C.   Alice Hemyngway daughter of George Hemyngway xped x^o die.
B.   Alice Booth buried xij^o die.
C.   Mary daughter of George Lumax xped xiij^o die.
B.   Will'm Bellabe buried eod. die.

January.

C.   George Bramham son of George Bramham xped ix^o die.
B.   An Hemyngway widow buried xxv^to die.

ffebruary.

M.   Will'm Nelson & Isabell Hallale married ij^o die.
C.   Mary Berridge daughter of Rob'rt Berridge xped vj^to die.
C.   Elizabeth Norman daughter Mr Will'm Norman xped xxvij^o die.

march.

C.   Thomas Hartley son of Thomas Hartley xped iiij^to die.
B.   William Leatham buried xij^mo die.

anno d'ni 1631 : regis : Car. 7.

aprill.

C.   Thomas son of John Claiton xped viij^o die.

may.

B.   Mary Berredge daughter of Robert Berredge buried vij^o die.
C.   William ffoister son of George ffoister xped xj^mo die.
B.   John Harrison buried eodem die pdct.
C.   Will'm Roundell son of Thomas Roundell xped xxxj^o die.

June.

B.   Jane Johnson wief of John Johnson buried xv^to die.
M.   Will'm Hemyngway and Margaret Wauld married xxj^mo die

July.

C. An Spink daughter of Thomas Spink xped xvij^{mo} die.

August vacat.

September.

B. Elizabeth daughter of Robert Walker buried j^{mo} die.
B. Thomas Elam buried xviij^o die.
C. Elizabeth Blakiston daughter of Mr Marmaduke Blakiston xped xxv^{to} die.
C. Jane the base daughter of John Lumbee xped eod : die.

October.

C. Bettrice daughter of An Leatham widow xped ix^o die.

November.

M. Matthew Bolton & Hellen Hill married xiij^o die.
C. An Nelson daughter of Will'm Nelson of Hillom Coppieholder xped xvj^{to} die.
B. Margaret wief of Giles Harrison buried xxix^o die.
C. Margaret Tutill daughter of George Tutill xped xxxm^o die.

december.

M. John Grime and Elizabeth Procter married xv^{to} die.

Januarie.

C. An Spinck daughter of George Spinck xped xxix^{no} die.

ffebruary.

C. Isabell bastard daughter of Thomas Carbee xped ij^{do} die.
C. An Spinck daughter of Godfrey Spinck xped
C. Richard Hemyngway son of Richard Hemyngway xped } v^{to} die.
B. doroty Bolton buried xx^{mo} die.
C. Hastings Ledsam son of John Ledsam xped xxij^o die.
B. Mary Ledsam wief of John Ledsam buried xxiij^o die.
C. George Watkin son of ffrancis Watkin xped eod xxiij die.
C. Elizabeth Barbar daughter of Will'm Barbar xped xxiiij^{to} die.

march.

C. Mary Burland bastard of Margaret Burland & John Elam xped xvj^{to} die.
C. ffrancis Walker son of Robert Walker xped xviij^o die.
C. Mary Turner daughter of Robert Turner xped xxj^{mo} die.

anno d'ni : 1632 : reg : car : Octavo.

B. Elizabeth wief of Henry Roundell buried xxvij^o die.
B. ffrancis Walker buried xxx^o die.
C. Will'm Green son of Rob'rt Green xped xxxj^{mo} die.
C. Hester dawson daughter of Randall dawson xped xxxj die.

aprill vacat.

may.

C. Jane Ryley daughter of Richard Ryley xped xiij^o die.
M. Bartholomew Longwood and An Simson married xxvij^o die.
C. doroty daughter of George Collier xped xxx^{mo} die.

June.

B. Mary Turner daughter of Robert Turner buried iiij^{to} die.
C. Mary Clean daughter of Will'm Clean xped xxiiij^o die.
B. Hastings Ledsam son of John Ledsam buried viij^o die.

C. John Lund son of Edward Lund xped viij⁰ die.
C. Margaret Guilliam daughter of George Guilliam xped xxij⁰ die.
C. Margaret Huscliff daughter of George Huscliff xped xxviij⁰ die.

september.

C. Stephen Pereson son of Michael Pereson xped xxv^to die.
C. An Roundel daughter of James Roundel xped xxx^mo die.

October.

C. James Bolton son of Matthew Bolton xped iiij^to die.
C. An Grime daughter of John Grime xped xvij⁰ die.
B. An Grime abovesaid buried xxij⁰ die.
B. An ffoister buried xxiiij⁰ die.

november.

C. Thomas Muse son of Nicolas Muse xped xj⁰ die.
C. Alice Blakiston daughter of Mr Marmaduke Blakiston xped xiij⁰ die.

december.

C. Thomas Hemyngway son of Will'm Hemyngway xped.
B. Jane Tutill buried xxx⁰ die.

January.

B. Hellen Browne buried x⁰ die.
C. John Wells son of Robert Wells xped xxv^to die.

ffebruarie.

B. Margaret Riley daughter of Richard Riley buried j^mo die.
B. Thomisin Roundel daughter of Thomas Roundel buried ij⁰ die.
M. John Hemyngway & Elizabeth Collier married xiiij^to die.

march.

C. Edmund Gylson son of John Gylson xped ij⁰ die And buried vj^to.
C. Jane Ledsam daughter of John Ledsam xped ⎫
C. John Illingwoorth son of John Illingwoorth xped ⎬ xvij⁰ die.
B. Will'm Walker son of Robert Walker buried xxiij⁰ die.

anno d'ni : 1633 : reg : car : nono.

aprill.

C. Katharine Spinck daughter of Godfrey Spinck xped v^to die.
B. Jane Norman wief of Roger Norman gent buried x⁰ die.
C. John Hubee son of Matthew Hubbee xped xiiij^to die.
B. Marget Crosley daughter of Peter Crosley buried xvj^to die.
C. An Bramham daughter of George Bramham xped xxij⁰ die.
B. Will'm ffoister son of George ffoister buried xxij⁰ die.
B. An Watkin wief of Antony Watkin buried xxxj^mo die.

may.

M. Peter Chappell and Mary Ralison (? Rawlison) married xxvj^to die.
C. Mary Shaw daughter of Will'm Shaw xped xxx^mo die.

June.

M. Dionise Clark & Prudence Barker married x⁰ die.
C. Robert Cut son of John Cut xped ⎫
C. Richard Tod son of John Tod xped ⎬ xvj^to die.
B. John Illingwoorth son of John Illingwoorth buried xviij die.

C. George Bew son of George Bew xped }
B. Mary daughter of Will'm Cocker buried } xxij⁰ die.
M. James Woode Isabel Karey married xxvto die.
B. Mary Nelson wief of ffrancis Nelson buried xxvij⁰ die.
C. Jane ffoister daughter of Thomas ffoister xped xxx⁰ die.

July.

B. Elizabeth Wells wief of George Wells buried xmo die.
M. John Robinson & An Smyth married xvjto die.
B. Sibill Selbee daughter of George Selbee buried xxiij⁰ die.

august.

C. Stephen Norman son of Mr Will'm Norman xped xjmo die.
C. Thomas Nelson son of Will'm Nelson xped }
M. Will'm Ellisse & An diconson married } xviij⁰ die.
                    September vacat.

october.

B. John Ward son of Isabell Ward widdow buried xv⁰ die.
C. Mary Claton daughter of John Claton xped xvij⁰ die.
B. Robert Howdell buried xviij⁰ die.
C. Luke Clark son of dionise Clark xped xviij⁰ die.
C. John Whale son of Nicolas Whale xped xx⁰ die.

november.

C. John Hartley son of Thomas Hartley xped xvij⁰ die.
M. Thomas Spinck and An Ward married xix⁰ die.

december.

C. ffrancis Muse son of Nicolas Muse buried ij⁰ die.
C. Robert Spinck son of Thomas Spinck xped xxij⁰ die.

January.

B. John ffitzrandall a Stranger buried xvjto die.
M. Cuthbert Bargh & An Robinson married xxiij⁰ die.

ffebruary.

B. ffrancis wief of Nicolas Hemyngway buried }
B. Margaret doughter of George Husclif buried } xiiij⁰ die.
B. William Cocker buried xix⁰ die.
B. Elizabeth daughter of ye said Will'm Cocker buried xxj⁰ die.

march.

C. Thomas Turner son of Rob'rt Turner xped ij⁰ die.
B. Tho: Turner aforesaid buried vijmo die.
C. John Lambert son of Thomas Lambert xped xvjto die.
C. Matthew Lund son of Edward Lund xped xxjmo die.

anno d'ni : 1634 reg. car : decimo.

B. John Lambard son of Thomas Lambert buried xxvij⁰ die.
C. An Wells daughter of Edward Wells xped xxxjmo die.

aprill.

C. Matthew son of George Hemyngway xped xxvto die.
C. George Gilson son of John Gilson xped }
C. John Cocker son of An Cocker xped }
C. Phillip son of John Barningham xped } xxvij⁰ die.
C. Elizabeth daughter of John Barningham xped }

may.

C. George Hemyngway son of Wᵐ Hemyngway xped ijº die.
B. Margaret Barker wief of Gervase Barker buried iiijᵗᵒ die.
C. Marmaduke Blakiston son of Mʳ Marmaduke Blakiston xped vjᵗᵒ die.
B. And yᵉ said Marmaduke Blakiston buried xiijº die.
C. Robert Spinck son of George Spinck xped xvᵗᵒ die.
B. George Hemyngway abovesaid buried xvᵗᵒ die.
C. George Illingwoorth son of John Illingwoorth xped xxvᵗᵒ die.
C. Isabel Walker daughter of Robert Walker xped ⎤
C. Alice Bolton daughter of Matthew Bolton xped ⎦ xxvijº die.
B. Antony Watkin buried xxixº die.

June.

M. ffrancis Nelson & Jane Blackburne married ⎤
B. John Whale son of Nicolas Whale buried ⎦ iijᵗⁱᵒ die
B. Alice daughter of John Illingwoorth buried xixº die.

July.

C. Robert Person son of John Pereson xped xiijº die.
M. Thomas Armestrong & ffrancis Mettham married xxxjº die.
C. Raertte Walker (?) son of George Wal (?) xped iii die.
M. John Berrie & Jane Atkinson married July the third.

august.

C. George son of George ffoister xped xxijº die.

september.

B. Mary daughter of Will'm Shaw buried jº die.

october.

C. John son of John Robinson xped jº die.
B. Margaret wief of Richard Bowling clerk buried ijº die A. Œtatis 86.
C. An daughter of Thomas Richardson xped iij die.
M. Brian Crosley & Elizabeth Snawsdayl married xxjº die.
C. An daughter of George Wauld xped xxviijº die.
C. An daughter of Thomas Loveday xped xxxº die.

november.

C. Jane daughter of John Cut xped xvjº die.
B. Margr't wief of Will'm Ingle buried xxiiij.
B. Thomas Pettinger buried xxvj die.
M. Will'm Swift & dorothy Blackburn married xxxº die.

december.

C. Margaret daughter of Matthew Hillingwoorth xped xº die.

January.

C. John son of Will'm Ellis xped xj die.
C. Grace daughter of George Wells xped xxjº die.
B. Alice wief of John Barningham buried xxx die.

ffebruary.

B. An wief of Thomas Brearcliff gent buried jº die.
C. Grace daughter of George Collier xped ixº die.
B. Phillip son of John Barningham buried xixº die.

march.

C. Peter son of Peter Chapple xped xviijth day.

anno d'ni : 1635 : reg : car 11º.

C. Elizabeth daughter of Edward Lund xped xxxº die.
B. George Selbee buried xxxjº die.

aprill.

C. Thomas son of John Beree junior xped xxxº die.

may.

C. Isabel daughter of Will'm Nelson of Hillom xped xijº die.
C. Rob'rt son of Rob'rt Turner xped xvijº die.
C. Margaret daughter of Mr Will'm Norman xped xxjº die.

June.

M. Leonard Smyth & Jenet Hallale married ij die.
C. Mary daughter of George Guilliam xped ⎫
C. William son of Nicolas Whale xped   ⎬ xxjº die.

July.

M. Seth Broadley & Jane Letham married xijº die.

august.

M. John Barmingham & Margr't Bocock married ijº die.
C. George son of Nicolas Muse xped ixº die.
B. John Johnson buried xxxjº die.

september.

C. Grace daughter of Will'm Swift xped xiijº die.
C. Tymothy son of George Bramham xped xxvijº die.

october.

B. Christofer Spinck buried viijº die.
B. Elizabeth daughter of John Barningham buried xvijº die.

november.

C. Peter son of Will'm Hemyngway xped jº die and buried.
C. John son of Will'm Bramham xped viij^{mo} die.
C. John son of John Ledsam xped xvº die.

december.

C. William son of Edward Wells xped jº die.
B. An Bramham widow buried ijº die.
C. Alice daughter of Michael Pereson xped xxvijº die.

January.

B. Margaret wief of Richard Grave buried xxiijº die.

ffebruary.

C. Posthumous son of Xpofer Spinck deceased xped vijº die.
C. Thomas son of Robert Walker xped xº die.
B. Katharine Rawlinson widdow buried xvº die.
B. Isabell wief of John Muse buried xviijº die.
B. Ursula Chambers widdow buried eod die.

march.

C. An daughter of Matthew Hubee xped x⁰ die.

anno d'ni 1636 : reg : car : 12.

Aprill.

C. An daughter of Thomas Spinck tanner xped xvᵗᵒ die.
M. John dobson & Catharine Chambers married xxiiijᵗᵒ die.
C. Mary daughter of John Robinson xped xxvjᵗᵒ die.
B. Mary Robinson abovesaid buried xxx⁰ die.

may.

C. John son of Nicolas dixson xped jᵐᵒ die.
B. Will'm Wells buried xx⁰ die.
C. John Tod son of John Tod xped xxij⁰ die.
M. Garvase Hebden & ffrancis Williamson married xxij⁰ die.

June.

C. Margaret daughter of Roᵬte Wels xped xij⁰ die.
B. Elizabeth wife of ffrancis Watkyn buried xv⁰ die.
C. Alvarey son of Mʳ Marmaduke Blakiston xped xix⁰ die

Julye.

B. William duffeild buried iij⁰ die.
B. John sonne of Thomas fflockton buried xxv⁰ die.

August.

C. Jane daughter of George Bewe xped xiiij⁰ die.
C. Elizabethe the bastard daughter of William Maysonne and Anne Harrisone as
    she confesseth and avereth xped eodem xiiij⁰ die.
C. William sonne of Charles Smith xped xiiij⁰ die.
B. John Pearsonne buryed the xxiij⁰ die.

September.

B. Richard Bowling Reader or Curate of this church buried the viijᵗʰ die, near ye
    sundiall on the Churchyard wall toward ye street or tower gate.

October.

C. Elizabeth Hemminway daughter of William Hem: xped: 2 die.
C. John Hartley sonne of Thomas Hartley xped vj die.

Nouember.

C. William sonne of Seath Bradley xped vj.
C. Anne Pearson daughter of John Pearson xped viij⁰ die.

December.

C. Auvarey sonne of Godfray Spink xped iiij die.
C. Elizabeth daughter of Robert Berridge xped xiij⁰ die.

Januarye.

C. Katharin daughter of John Berrie xped vij die.
C. ffrancis sonne of

ffebruary.

C. Mary daughter of George Hemmingway xped 12 die.
C. Elizabeth daughter of Thomas Richinson xped xviij die.

C. Margerit Welles daughter of Robert Well xped xxvj die.
B. Nicolas Hemminway sonne of Robert Buried the v die.
B. Sisley Colliare Buried the 8 die.

Anno domini 1637 : Reg : Char : 13.

March.

B. William Roundall sonne of Thomas Roundall buried the xxviijº.

May.

C. Margaret daughter of John Claton xped the xj die.
M. Roger Northine & Urseley Sellby maried xiiijº die.

June.

C. William sonne of John Robinson xped vj^th die.
B. Anne Webster daughter of Robert Webster buryed the xij die.
B. William sonne of George Cholliare buried the xxij die.
C. Richard sonne of Richard Rylay xped xxiiij die.

August.

C. Anne daughter of Mr William Norman xped xxij die.

September.

B. Sisley Colliar buried v^th die.
C. Beniamin sonne of Thomas Candie xped vj die.
C. Samuell sonne of Peter Chapple xped xvij die.
M. John Brame and Jane Addingson married the xxiiij die.

October.

C. Isabell daughter of Thomas Mewse xped i2 die.
M. Thomas Clarke and Ailsce Sympson married xvij^th die.
C. Jane daughter of George Welles xped xviij^th die.

November.

C. William Cleane sone of William cleane xped 19 die.
C. Rebeca spincke doughter of Thomas spincke xped 26 die.
C. An Turner doughter of Robart Turner xped 29 die.

Januarii.

B. ffrancis Roundill doughter of Thomas xiij die.
B. Jane Hollingworth wief of Mathew xxvj die.

ffebruarii.

B. George Wauld son of George iij die.
C. ffrances Quall son of Nickolas xj die.
C. Margrit Snawesdall daughter of Arcillas xj die.
C. Mathias Spinke sonn of George xped x day.

March.

M. Ann Gillyam daughter of George buried ij die.
B. Joan Bery buryed the v die.
M. Richard Harricion buryed the iij die.
C. Bastard chilld of George Tomlinson xped j die.

Anno domini 1638.

C. ffrancis daughter of Thomas Clarke xxvij^th die.

12

Aprill.

B. Matthew dawson buried the vth day.
C. Jane daughter of John Illingworth the 12 day.
C. George sonne of Thomas ffoyster the 17th day.
C. Mary daughter of William Bramham the 29th day.

July.

C. Anne daughter of Rob'rt Berridge the vth day.

August.

C. Mary daughter of John Ledsome the 20th day.

September.

B. George Waud the 27th day.
B. Robert Webster sonne of Robert Webster the 29th day.

Nowember.

C. Jane daughter of Nicolas dicson the 17th day.
B. John sonne of John Robinson the 18th day.
B. William Brume the 8th day.

Nowember.

B. Jane Ledsom daughter of John Ledsome the 2^d.

december.

C. Jane daughter Robert Walker the 7.

January.

C. Elizabeth daughter of George Bramham the 16th day.
M. John dawson and Issabell Hemmingway the 17.

ffebruary.

M. Robert Cockell and Jane Waud the first day.
M. Andrewe Clarke and Anne ffocton the 17th day.
C. Edmond sonne of Richard Hall the 15th day.
C. Elizabeth daughter of Richard Stubbes the 24 day.

March.

C. George Spinke sone of Godfray Spinke the first day.
B. George sonne of William Atkinson the 8 day.

Anno domini 1639.

B. Sammuell sonne of Peter Chappell the 3j day.

Aprill.

C. William Ramsden sonne of William Ramsden armi: the 8th day.
C. Robert sonne of Andrewe Clarke the 10 day.
B. Thomas Clarke the 24th day.
B. Chatheran daughter of John Berridge the 24th day.
B. ffrancis a bastard child of Jane Wike the 26th day.

may.

B. Michaell pearson the 5th day.
C. Elizabeth daughter of John Tod the 5th day.
B. Jane daughter of John Illingworth the 13th.

}. Richard of George Wawker the 14th day.
}. Sarah daughter of M*r* Burdet the 16th day.

June.

}. John Braime sonne of John Braime the 17th day.
}. Jane Hallelay buried the 19th day.
}. William sonne of William Ramsden the 29th day.

Julie.

}. Nicholas Leatham the 24th day.
}. William Ramsden buried the 8th day.
}. Hercules Snawsdell the 29th day.

August.

{. John Lumbie and Alce Spoffard the 7th day.

September.

}. Thomas Nutter buried the 3d day.
}. Jane daughter of Hercules Snawsdell the 3d day.
:. Chatharine daughter of William Hemmingway the 15th day.
}. dorothie wife to George Spinke the 17th day.
:. Matthew sonne of John Lumbie the 22d day.
:. Edward sonne of John Robinson the 29th day.

October.

}. Elizabeth daughter of Alce Pearson the 29th
}. Nicholas Waud buried the 18th day.
:. Thomas sonne of William Ellis the 20 day.

Nouember.

:. Benjamin sonne of Thomas Camdidge the 3d day.
:. Matthew sonne of George Guilliam 19th day.

Januarie.

}. Anne Bellaby the 6 day.
}. Richard sonne of John Tod the 19 day.

March.

}. Jane Cleane wife to William Cleane the 3d day.
:. George Lauacocke (Lavacocke) sonne of John Lau: the 9th day of ffebruarie.
:. Zacharie sonne of Robert Gambie the 22nd day.
:. Mary daughter of George Wells the 22d day.
}. Alce Pearson Widowe the 14th day.

March 1640.

}. Martin Harryson buried the 26t day.

Aprill.

}. Richard sonne of Richard Riley the 8th day.
:. Elizabeth daughter of John Illingworth the 3d day.

May.

}. Thomas sonne of Robert Walker the 22d day.
}. George ffoyster the 22d day.

June.

B. ffrancis daughter of Thomas Clarke the 3ᵈ day.
C. Mary daughter of Edward Lund the 11th day.
C. Anne daughter of Nicholas Welles the 24th day.
B. Thomas Varay the 24th day.
C. Jane daughter of William Bell the 28t day.

July.

C. William sonne of Thomas Clarke the 19th day.

August.

C. Sarah daughter of William Norman the 6t day.

September.

B. John sonne of William Norman the 22ᵈ day.

October.

B. James Roundell buried the vth day.
C. Robert sonne of Robert Walker the 28 day.

Nouember.

C. John sonne of William Mason the 4th day.
C. Jane daughter of William Swift the ij day.

december.

C. Thomas sonne of Thomas Nordon (?) the 20 day.
C. Rebecha daughter of John Berrie the 22 day.

January.

B. Giles Harrison buried the 8 day.
C. Margaret daughter of William Bramman.

ffebruarye.

C. Sarah daughter of Thomas Spinke the 21th (or 3jtb) day of January.
C. Alce daughter of John Pearson the 2ᵈ day.
B. Elizabeth daughter of John Tod the ij day.
B. Alce Illingworth daughter of John Illing: the 16th day.
B. Thomas sonne of ffrancis Nelson the 19th day.
B. William Burton the 20th day.
M. William Cleane and Elizabeth Webster the 24th day.

march.

C. Peter sonne of William Hemmingway 2ᵈ day.
C. Anne daughter of John Bell the 16th day.
B. Anne daughter of Matthew Hewby the 16 day.

Anno domini 1641.

B. William Roundell the 25th day.

Aprill.

C. Elizabeth daughter of John Lumby xped the 4.

June vacat.

C. Jane daughter of Robert Turner the 4th day.
B. Richard Democke quarter maister the 6th day.
C. Joseph of John Claton the 2j day.

July.

B. Isabell wife of Ralph Norton buried ye 2 of July.

Januarie Ano d'ni 1642.

C. Beniamin Spinke sonne of Thomas Spinke xped the first day.
B. Rob't Nutt Buried the 26th day.

ffebruary.

B. Alice Pereson doughter to John Pereson Buried the 29th.

July Ann. Domi 1642.

C. Peter Burnit son of Mr Witles? Burnit baptized xvj.
March vacat.

Aprill Ano d'mi 1644.

Joseph & Benjamin sonnes of Godfrey Spinke xped ye 20 of Aprill 1644. Bur:
B. david Hallelay buried the 24th day.
B. Ann Richardson doughter to Thomas Richardson buried the 30th day.

may.

B. mary the daughter of Will'm Hemingway borne about this time.
Jenet daughter to Rob't Bew buried the 20° die.

June.

B. Saray daughter to Thomas Spinke buried the 8th day.

July. August. September.

B. Rob't sonne of Thomas Harrison buried the 27th day of July.
B. Jane Mewse daughter of Nicholas Mewse the last of July.
B. Elizabeth Northen daughter of Thomas Northen ye 2^d of August.
C. Elizabeth daughter of William Adkinson the 18th of August.
B. John Robinson buried ye 12th of September.
Sep^ber.
B. Duke sonne of Charles Smith buried ye 26 of September.

October. Nouember.

B. John sonne of John Illingworth buried ye 16 of October.
C. Elizabeth daughter of John Dawson xped ye 3 of Nouember.
C. Julian doughter of Robert Sommers xped ye 13 of Nouember.
B. Ales daughter of Robert Cockill buried ye 13 of Nouember.
C. Thomas sonn of Thomas Hasle xped ye 24 of Nouember.

december.

B. Thomas sonn of George Wells buried ye 20 of December.
C. Bartholemew sonn of Barth: fflecher xped the 19 of December.
C. Elizabeth daughter of Thomas Hunter xped the 20 of December.
M. Thomas Lambe and Ursula married ye 28 of December.

January.

B. Thomas sonn of Thomas Johnson buried ye 4 of January.
C. John sonn of Robert Wright xped ye 19 of January.
B. Anna Smith wife of Charles Smith buried ye 21 of January.

ffebruary.

C. Beniamin sonn of Thomas mewse xped ye 2 of ffebruary.
M. Will Hallelay and Sara Ingam married ye 13 of ffebruary.

march.

C. George sonn of Thomas Herby xped ye 5th of march.
B. George sonn of Thomas Herby buried ye 7th of march.
C. John sonn of John Lawerocke xped ye 18 of march.
M. Laurence Benson & Sara Dussen married ye 24th of march.

march 1645.

C. Anna daughter of Thomas Backhouse xped ye 29 of march.
C. margarett daughter of John Hart xped ye 30 of march.

Aprill.

C. William sonn of Thomas Osburne xped ye 3 of Aprill.
C. John sonn of John Person xped ye 4th of Aprill.
C. Will sonn of Will Pease xped ye 5th of Aprill.
C. Anna daughter of Thomas Hagh xped ye 5 of Aprill.
C. Mary daughter of Will Gilliam xped ye 5 of Aprill.

April 1645.

M. William Watson and Ellin Skelton married ye 8 of Aprill.
C. John Greenwood sonn of Mr John Greenwood minister of this church ye 10 of Aprill.
C. Jane daughter of Phillip Camage xped ye 10 of April.
B. Elizabeth daughter of John Illingworth buried ye 13 of April.
C. Anna daughter of Thomas Joneson xped ye 13 of April.
C. Anna daughter of Will Bilton xped ye 24 of Aprill.

may.

C. Godfrey sonne of John Hainar xped ye 4th of may.
C. John sonn of John Vincent xped ye 4th of may.
C. Godfrey sonn of Godfrey Robucke xped ye 7th of may.
C. Anna Lecham daughter of John Lecham xped ye 7th of may.
B. Jane Cockell wife of Robert Cockell buried ye 18th of may.
M. John West & margarett Cawood married ye 22th of may.
C. mary daughter of Gabriell Bramham xped ye 29th of may.

June.

C. George sonn of Richard Turner xped ye 6th of June.
C. Richard sonn of William Hemingway xped ye 13th of June.
C. Godfry sonn of Elias Hallelay xped ye 18th of June.

July.

C. mary and Anna Wells daughters of George Wells xped ye 4th of July.
M. Peter Banett (? Barrett) & mary ffreeman married ye 8th of July.
B. mary daughter of George Wells Buried ye 8th of July.
B. Anna Wells daughter of George Wells Buried ye 13 of July.
M. Edward Walker and Alice Conney married ye 18 of July.
C. mary daughter of Thomas Harrison xped ye 18 of Julie.
C. William sonn of Edward Bradley xped ye 13 of Julie.

August.

M. George Spinke and Jane Nutt married 1th of August.
C. mary daughter of William mason xped ye 5 of August.
C. Elizabeth daughter of John Hardwicke ye 7th of August.
M. Thomas Smith & ffrancis Smith married ye 7th of August.
C, Will. sonn of Will Boocock xped ye 10th of August.

Elizabeth daughter of Thomas Clarke xped ye 24 of August.
John son of Will Cidane xped ye 24th of August.
John Hemingway buried the 24th of August.

September vacat

October.

Anna daughter of Thomas Richardson xped ye 26th of October.
Will. Barbar buried ye 29th of October.
Jarvas sonn of Edward Haggs xped ye 31 of October.

november.

Thomas Willson & mary Short married ye 1th of november.
Jaruas sonn of Edward Haggs buried ye 2 of november.
Mary daughter of Thomas Robinson buried ye 7th of nouember.
Naphtali sonn of Naphtali Brasebricke xped ye 13 of nowember.
Richard Graues (Graves) buried ye 14th of nouember.

Nouember 1645.

Elizabeth daughter of Mr John Stanford xped ye 18th of november.
John Hvett (? Huett) and Elizabeth King married ye 27th of nouember.
Richard Sheaperd & Sara Hepden married ye 30th of nouember.

December.

mary daughter of Will. Richardson xped ye 1th of December.
Elizabeth daughter of Edward Clarke xped ye 7th of December.
Will sonn of Richard Hallelah xped ye 21th of December.
Will sonn of Will Ruet xped ye 28th of December.

January.

James sonn of Thomas Robinson xped ye 8th of January.
ffrancis daughter of Richard Hall xped ye 9th of January.
Anna daughter of John Battman xped ye 21 of January.
Jennett daughter of Will. Abbott xped ye 28 of January.

ffebruary.

John sonn of Mr Godfry Sommersell xped ye 2 of ffebruary.
William Reare and Elizabeth Butterfield married ye 5 of ffebruary.
John dale and Dorithy Webster married ye 10 of ffebruary.
Will sonn of John Jackson xped ye 16th of ffebruary.
Cristopher sonn of Nicolas daniell xped ye 16 of ffebruary.
Dinah Daughter of Cristopher Marrham xped ye 17 of ffebruary.
Edith daughter of John Redchester xped ye 17 of ffebruary.
Ambrose sonn of John Godson xped ye 17 of ffebruary.
Anne daughter of Paull Tompson xped ye 22 of ffebruary.
Anna daughter ffrancis Katteson xped ye 26 of ffebruary.

march.

Thomas sonn of Thomas Welles xped ye 1 of march.
Thomas sonn of Roger Bolton xped ye 7 of march.
Will sonn of John Sugden xped ye 8 of march.
Thomas Abbott and Mary Chappell married ye 8 of march.
Will son of Will Tompsonn xped ye 11th of march.
Anna daughter of James Butler xped ye 11th of march.
Mr Robert Davell buried ye 16 of march.
John Shilleto and Cicely Pease married ye 30 of march.
John Abbott and Isabella Drury married ye 31 of march.
Richard Paule and Elizabeth Harrison married ye 31 of march.

1646.
Aprill.

M. Thomas Reame and margarett Wood married ye 14 of Aprill.
M. Luke middleton & Ester Berredge married ye 16 of Aprill.
C. margarett daughter of John mabbey xped ye 20 of Aprill.

may.

C. Will sonn of Thomas Nutte xped ye 1th of may.
C. John sonn of Thomas Haigh xped 12 of may.
C. ffrances daughter of John ffaburne xped ye 13 of may.
M. Robert Thackarah and Ellin Cooke married ye 14 of may.
C. Thomas sonn of John West xped ye 23 of may.
B. An Infant of the said John West buried ye same day.
C. Anna daughter of Andrew Clarke xped ye 24 of may.
M. Will Brooke and Elizabeth Cooke married ye 27 of may.
B. Isabella Abram buried ye 31 of may.

June.

C. John sonn of Thomas Hasley xped ye 12 of June.
C. Mary daughter of Edward Walker xped ye 16 of June.

July.

C. Elizabeth daughter of Will Brooke xped ye 5 of July.
C. James sonn of Will Todd xped ye 5 of July.
M. John Wells & Alice Clarke married ye 7 of July.

August.

C. Elizabeth daughter of Henry Mather xped ye 3 of August.
M. Lawrance Hide & Elizabeth Anderson married ye 3 of August.
M. Henry Abbott & Alice Hallelay married ye 5 of August.
B. Alice wife of Mr George Norman buried the 18 of August.
M. John Middleton and Isabell Turpen married ye 12 of August.
C. Elizabeth daughter of John Vincent xped ye 16 of August.
M. Will Lee and Bridgett Barker married ye 17 of August.
C. James sonn of John Turpen xped ye 24 of August.
C. Elizabeth daughter of Will Bramham xped 26 of August.

September.

B. John sonn of Will Cleane buried ye 11 of September.
C. Henry sonn of Henry Joneson xped ye 13 of September.
B. Alice daughter of John morley buried ye 14 of September.

October.

B. Thomas sonn of Thomas Nutter buried ye 3 of October.
C. Alice daughter of John Ledsam xped ye 4 of October.
M. Mr John Willson and Mrs Anna Clough married ye 12 of October.
C. Elizabeth daughter of Robert Wright xped 14 of October.
C. Will sonn of Will Smith xped ye 15 of October.
C. dennis sonn of John Wells xped ye 18 of October.

november.

M. Mathew Basebeck and Elizabeth Poules married 4 of november.
C. Thomas sonn of Will Bolton xped ye 8 of november.
M. Edward Lunnd and Katharin Bell married ye 19 of nouember.

B.   An Infant buried of Richard Turners yᵉ 22 of nouember.
M.   Richard Backhouse and Elizabeth Whitwood married yᵉ 23 of november.
C.   John sonn of Will Camdidge xped yᵉ 29 of november.

December.

B.   Jane daughter of Charles Smith buried yᵉ 16 of December.
C.   Jane daughter of Robert Hallelay xped yᵉ 17 of December.
C.   Elizabeth daughter of Thomas Letham xped yᵉ 26 of december.
C.   Thomas sonn of John Shilleto xped yᵉ 28 of December.

January.

C.   Will son of George Wells xped yᵉ 10 of January.
M.   Will Simpson & Mary Hubie married yᵉ 20ᵗʰ day.
M.   Brian Daniell and ffrances Graves married yᵉ 26 of January.

ffebruary.

M.   John Huby and Mary Hollinworth married yᵉ 2 ffebruary.
M.   John Hollingworth & Elizabeth Berry married yᵉ 9 of ffebruary.
B.   Jane wife of Seth Broadly buried yᵉ 11 of ffebruary.
C.   Anna daughter of Thomas Procter xped yᵉ 14 of ffebruary.
C.   Will sonn of Luke middleton xped yᵉ 14 of ffebruary.
M.   Edward Procter and Mary Lee married yᵉ 17 of ffebruary.
C.   matthew sonn of Edward haggs xped yᵉ 24 of ffebruary.
M.   Cudbart Hallelay & Jennett Haton married yᵉ 25 of ffebruary.

march 1647.

M.   William Tomlinson & Mary Norman married yᵉ 1 of march.
C.   Will sonn of Timothy Bramham xped yᵉ 14 of march.
C.   William sonn of Mʳ William Gamble xped yᵉ 25 of march.

Aprill.

C.   Thomas sonn of John Lund xped yᵉ 10 of Aprill.
M.   Robert Jenkinson and Joane Rewell married yᵉ 20 of Aprill.

may.

B.   Anna daughter of Thomas Procter buried yᵉ 9 of may.
M.   Mʳ Henry Ramsdem and Mˢ margarett Aclam married yᵉ 28 of may.
C.   Augustine sonn of John Sauage xped yᵉ 29 of may.
C.   Alice daughter of Will Massy xped yᵉ 29 of may.

June.

C.   Mary daughter of William Daniell xped yᵉ 3 of June.
C.   Elizabeth daughter of Henry Abbots xped 16 of June.
M.   Will. draper and Jane Steney married yᵉ 28 of June.

July.

B.   Jane wife of Will Nelson buried yᵉ 1 of July.
B.   Thomas Ereby buried yᵉ 3 of July.
M.   marten Ramsden and Elizabeth Colson married yᵉ 8 of July.
M.   George Burne and Jennett Roberts married yᵉ 27 of July.
M.   Mar Gilliam & Anna Reynord yᵉ 27 of July.

August.

B.   Jennett wife of John Berry buried yᵉ 2 of August.
M.   Robert Herrison and Katherin Morton married yᵉ 3 of August.

13

B.   John Procter buried yᵉ 17 of August.
C.   Will son of Robert Turner xped yᵉ 29 of August.

September.

C.   John sonn of Mʳ John Wilson xped the 2 of September.
M.   Alexander Tauendar and Margarett Brigge married 4 Sbʳ.
M.   William Smith and Margarett Bocock married 23 Seƥber.
C.   Elizabeth daughter of Edward Bradly xped yᵉ 26 of September.
M.   Gabriell Bramham & Anna Howdell married yᵉ 29 of September.

October.

C.   William sonn of Thomas Smith xped yᵉ 1 of October.
M.   Richard Roundell & Anna Stockill married yᵉ 11 of October.
C.   Mary davghter of Mʳ John Greenwood xped yᵉ 12 of October.
M.   Anthony Hudson and Anna Short married yᵉ 18 of October.
M.   Walter Benson and Elizabeth Gilliam married yᵉ 19 of October.
B.   John sonn of John Lauerock buried yᵉ 26 of October.
M.   Robert Hall and Margarett Lee married yᵉ 26 of October.
M.   John Lee and Alice dawson married yᵉ 26 of October.
C.   William son of .... Stanforth Christned.

november.

M.   Laurence .... and Merriall ffletcher married 1 november.
M.   William Skelton & Anna .... married yᵉ 8 of nouember.
C.   John sonn of Thomas Harrison xped yᵉ 8 of nouember.
M.   Richard Wheldrick and Jennett ffeaton married yᵉ 11 november.
C.   Will sonn of John Vincent xped yᵉ 12 of nouember.
M.   Jaruas Hauton & Jane Tomplinson married yᵉ 18 november.
B.   Jane West buried yᵉ 18 of nouember.
M.   John Wright & Elizabeth Crawshaw married 20 nouember.
B.   John Lund Buried yᵉ 25 of nouember.
M.   Will Berry and Jane Gilson married yᵉ 30 of nouember.

december.

C.   Mary daughter of Richard Turner xped yᵉ 10 of december.
B.   Elizabeth wife of John Hemingway buried yᵉ 13 of december.
C.   Thomas son of George Bew junior xped yᵉ 19 of december.
C.   ffrances a bastard of Jarvas Hautons xped yᵉ 19 of december.
C.   Elizabeth daughter of John Batman xped yᵉ 19 of december.

January.

M.   George Harbottle & Elizabeth Whalley married yᵉ 2 of January.
B.   Thomas sonn of George Bew jun buried yᵉ 2 of January.
B.   Jarvas Barker buried yᵉ 13 of January.
C.   John sonn of Edward Procter xped yᵉ 26 of January.

ffebruary.

M.   James Webster and Anna Rodwell married yᵉ 1 of ffebruary.
C.   Anna daughter of Will Adkinson xped yᵉ 10 of ffebruary.
M.   Thomas Leake & ffrances Burton married yᵉ 14 of ffebruary.
C.   mary daughter of John mabee xped yᵉ 24 of ffebruary.
C.   John sonn of James Butler xped yᵉ 24 of ffebruary.
C.   Alice a Bastard of Thomas Thomsons xped yᵉ 24 of ffebruary.

march.

B.   margarett wife of Robert Hall buried yᵉ 3 of march.
     John sonn of Will Cowper xped yᵉ 12 of march.

Ann daughter of Richard northen xped ye 16 of march.
mary daughter of George Burne xped ye 29 of march.

Aprill 1648.

. Will Bankam and . . . . . . married 3 of Aprill.
. Katherin daughter of Robert wright xped ye 4 of Aprill.
. Elizabeth wife of George Tutill buried ye 5 of Aprill.
. John sonn of Thomas Procter xped ye 16 of April.
. Margarett daughter of John Huby xped ye 19 of Aprill.
. Richard Hardwicke & Elizabeth Hemingway married 20 of Aprill.
. George Bramham buried ye 28 of Aprill.

May.

. Robert Holdhead & Mary Chambers married 12 of May.
. Anna daughter of Roger Bolton xped ye 17 of May.
. John Chapman & Elizabeth Perkins married ye 25 of May.
. Margarett wife of Robert Webster buried ye 26 of May.

June.

. John sonn of William Berry xped ye 14 of June.
. Robert & Alice twinns of John Person xped ye 18 of June.
Edmund sonn of Edward Lund xped ye 24 of June.
. Thomas Illingworth & Anna Wells married ye 25 of June.
. George sonn of Will Shaw xped ye 30 of June.

July.

. Richard sonn of Robert Herrison xped ye 29 of July.
. Will son of George Welkes xped ye 28 of July.

August.

. Mary daughter of Thomas Townend xped ye 1 of August.
. Anthony Heptonstall & Elizabeth Savre married 3 August.
. Elizabeth Berrie daught of John Berrie xped the eighteenth of August. [This entry is erased in the Register.]
. Mary daughter of George Ansewoorth xped ye 14 of August.
. John sonne of Edward Clarke bapt.
. Joseph Nellson & Mary Procter married ye 22 of August
. Thomas Turton & Elizabeth Taylor married ye 28 of August.

September.

. Alice daughter of Will Rust xped ye 17 of September.

October.

. Thomas sonn of Thomas Robinson xped ye 14 of October.
. Richard sonn of Gabriell Bramham xped ye 17 of October.
. John sonn of John Clarke xped ye 24 of October.

December 1648.

. John Berrie and Ann Shillito married the 27.

ffebruary.

Sara daughter of Mr John Greenwood xped ye 27 of ffebruary.

1649.

. John sonne of Robert Halliley.
. Thomas sonne of Thomas Leetham bapt August 16.

C. Thomas sonne of John Bingley bap^t September 27.
B. John dawson of Hilham buryed July 4.
B. Jane daughter of Nicholas dixin buryed ⎫
   Elizabeth daughter of Seth Broadley buryed ⎰ October 19th
C. Anne daughter of George Bew Junior of Hilham december.
M. Edward Grant & Elizabeth .... marryed.

Anno. 1650.

C. Robert sonne of Thomas Harrison bap^t April 16.
C. John sonne of Mr John Stanford bap^t April 24.
M. William Allen of Kellington and Mary Nutt June 24.
M. William Banes and Alice Hollingworth July 10.
C. Mary daughter of Edward Clark.
B. Elizabeth Hollingworth vid buryed August 20.
C. Elizabeth daughter of John Bary.
C. Elizabeth daughter of Edward Grant August 25.
C. Mary daughter of George Wells Nouember 7.
C. Richard sonne of Luke Middleton bap^t december 23.
C. Mary daughter of Marmaduke Gilliam bap^t december 26.
C. Richard sonne of George Harbottle bap^t december 27.
B. James Hollingworth buryed January 17.

C. Thomas sonne of Arthur Hamon bap^t January	19
B. Ellen wife of Ralph Dobson buryed ffebruary	2
C. Anne daughter of Thomas Robinson bap^t February	6
C. Mary daughter of John West bap^t	22
C. Henry sonne of John Leetham of Milford bap^t	26
B. Infant of Thomas Richardson buryed february	27

C. Thomas sonne of Bartholomew Hollingworth bap^t March 21.

1651.

C. Isabel daughter of Richard Roundell bap^t March	27
B. .... sonne of Thomas Daniel (?) buryed	28

C. .... sonne of Richard Shearcroft of Lumby bap^t April first.

C. William sonne of Mr Thomas Norman bap^t May	16
B. Anne ffrandelrand Widdow buryed	8
B. John sonne of Thomas Clarke buried	9
B. Anne daughter of Walter Benson buryed	23
C. Margaret daughter of Robert Harrison bap^t	25
C. Elizabeth daughter of Timothie Bramham bap^t June	26

B. George Lumax buryed.   -
C. John son of Thomas Richardson baptized Febr 24.
C. Bartholemew sonne of John Linsdall bap^t October 16.
C. Anne daughter of Bartholemew Bramham bap^t 22.

B. Jennet daughter of Richard Ryley buryed december	10
C. Mary daughter of Mr Richard Rider bap^t	27
C. Michael sonne of Michael Coolen bap^t January	1
C. Isaac sonne of Mr William Gamble bap^t	2
C. Henry sone of Thomas dicken bap^t february	2
C. Patience daughter of Edward Lund baptized	18
B. Elizabeth daughter of George Lummax buryed febr.	4
B. Thomas sonne of John Pierson buryed	22
B. Elizabeth daughter of .... Lumby buryed March	7
B. Ralph Dobson buryed March	8
B. Robert Leaper of friston buryed	10

Alice wife of Thomas Clarke buryed

C. Margaret daughter of Mr John Stanforth bap^t March	16
B. Anne wife of Phillip Cammidge buryed	19

B.	Edith Halliley vid. buryed Nouember	14
C.	.... sonne of Henry Harryson of Lumby bapt	15
M.	Henry Stanige & Anne Spinke marryed Nouember	18
M.	John Wilson and Isabell Hollingworth married	27
M.	Thomas Wentforth & Elizabeth Spinke marryed december	10
B.	Robert Hemingway of Hilham buried	14

1652.

C.	John sonne of Edward Walker bapt.	
C.	William sonne of Edward Grant.	
B.	Elizabeth wife of Robert Craven buryed april	2
C.	.... daughter of John Bingley bapt.	
C.	Anne daughter of Wm Hemingway baptized	15
B.	George Walker buryed June	12
M.	John Oxleye Jane Hanley marryed	22
M.	James Brooke & Elizabeth Norman marryed June	29
C.	Mary daughter of George Bew of Hilham bapt July	6
M.	John Barker and Elizabeth Hemingway married	8
C.	William son of Ralph ffeaton bapt July	11
C.	Thomas sonne of William Wheldrake bapt	11
B.	Jennett wife of William Atkinson burried	14
C.	William sonne of Thomas Harrison bapt	20
C.	Robert sonne of Robert Craven bapt August	8
C.	Mary daughter of Joseph Nelson bapt	29
B.	Susan wife of George Gilliam buryed September	6
C.	Jane daughter of Edward Procter bapt	9
C.	George Waud sonne of ffrancis Waud bapt. October	14
M.	Arthur Topcliffe & Elizabeth Tutill married	20
B.	Henry dickson a stranger buryed Nouember	4
C.	William sonne of Robert Halliley bapt	7
C.	Richard sonne of George Browne bapt	9
C.	John sonne of Andrew Clarke bapt	21
C.	Christopher sonne of John Sawer bapt	25
C.	John sonne of Thomas Leatham bapt december	2
C.	Richard sonne of Edward Hudson bapt	2
C.	Jennett daughter of Robert Bramham bapt	5
M.	Robert Brashaw and Jane Hodgsonn marryed January	6
C.	Anne daughter of Marmaduke Gilliam bapt	25
C.	Elizabeth daughter of Mr Thomas Norman bapt ffebruary	2
C.	Thomas sonne of Thomas Bateman bapt	2
M.	George Lanceley and Ellener Markeham married	10
C.	Elizabeth daughter of Richard Procter bapt	20
B.	ffrancis wife of Jarvise Hebden buryed March	17
C.	Anne darkgter of Henry dickson bapt	20
B.	Jane daughter of Phillip Cammidge buryed	22
C.	Thomas sonne of John Oxeley bapt	23

1653.

C.	Mary daughter of Michael Coolen bapt March	24
C.	James sonne of Bartholemew Hollingworth bapt	29
C.	Elizabeth daughter of George Harbottle bapt April	20
C.	Margaret daughter of John Barker bapt May	4
C.	Matthew sonne of Mr Mathew Hall bapt	12
C.	Richard sonne of Arthur Hammond bapt	19
B.	Leonard Bustard buryed June	9
C.	Sara daughter of John Berry bapt July	3
B.	William Berry buryed	14

B. John Hubie buryed   16
B. Katherine wife of Thomas Leathem buryed   31
B. William sonne of Mr William Gamble buryed August   25
B. Alice daughter of Michael Pearson buryed September   6
B. Margaret wife of William Nettleton buryed   10
C. William base sonne of Wm Rumans & Sara Whiteley bap^t 11
C. Jeremiah sonne of William Hemingway bap^t   12
B. Anne ffarrer widdow buryed   October   3
B. Elizabeth Leatham widdow buryed   8
C. Jane daughter of Arthur Topliffe bap^t   9
B. Jane daughter of Robert Halliley buryed   10
B. Jeremiah sonn of William Hemmingway bap^t   16
C. John Cockill sone of Robt. Cockill borne the 9 of November.
B. Jennet daughter of Robt. Turner buried the 17 of December.
C. Elizabeth Daughter of Thomas Robinson borne the 19
C. Thomas son of Thomas Dickon borne the   19
C. William son of Will'm Barnes (?) borne the 4 of January.
C. Marÿ Daughter of Richard Smyth borne the 5 of January.
C. John sone of Edward Walker borne the seventh of ffebruary.
C. Thomas Spinke sone of John Spinke baptized eight.
C. Thomas sone of Thomas Lepington borne   13
B. Thomas ffoister buried the   22
C. Elizabeth Daughter of Bartholomew Bramham borne ye 26
C. Elizabeth Daughter of Edward Thachthat borne the 8 of March.
C. Jane Daughter of ffrancis Waude borne the sixteenth.
B. Thomas son of Tymothy Bramham buried the   21

1654.

C. Marke sone of Marke Parker A Souldier borne the 16 of April.
C. Edward sone of John Linsdale borne the 12 of Maÿ.
C. William sonne of Robert Harrison borne the 27 of Maÿ.
B. William sone of Robert Harrison buried the 3^d of June.

Bee it remembered that John Berrie of Monckfriston was sworn before John Odingsale, of Rest Parke Esquire one of the Justices of peace for the West Ridinge to execute the office of A pish Register for the pish of Monckfriston Hyllam & Burton upon the ffourth Day of May. 1654.

Jo: Odingsels.

Be it remembred y^t Michael Gilliam of ye parishe of Shirburne and Elizabeth Powel? of ye parish of Monkfriston were married before John Odingsels of Rest Parke one of ye Justices of peace for ye West Ridding according to ye Act of Parliament upon ye 4 of May. 1654.

Jo: Odingsels.

Be it remembred that Anthonÿ Hepinstall and Margaritt Jackson both of the pish of Monckfriston were married before John Ward of Tanchill one of the Justices of peace for the West Riddinge according to the Act of Parliament the sixt of Maÿ. 1654.

Jo: Warde

Be it remembred that Brian Thomlinson of the pish of Monkfriston and Katharne Perkin of Gateforth in pish of Braton were married before John Odingsale of Reast Parke in the County of Yorke one of the Justices of the peace for the West Riddinge according to the Act of Parliament the eighteenth of May: 1654.

Jo: Odingsels.

Be it remembred that John Nelson of the pish of Monkfriston And Issabell Pullan of the Parish of Ledsam were married before me John Odingsels of Reast Parke Esquire one of the Justices of the West Ridinge accordinge to the Act of Parliament in the yeare of our Lord 1653 upon the one and thirteth day of July 1654.

Jo: Odingsels.

Be it Rememberd that John Oxley & Mary Shereing both of Burton w^{thin} the parish of Monkfryston were married before John Warde of Tanshelfe (According to an Act of Parliament in that case made) upon the nineth day of September 1654.

Jo: Warde.

Be it Remembred that John Bustard of Monckfryston and Eliz Gybson of Kippax were married before me John Ward of Tanshill Accordinge to the Act of Parliament in that Case made upon the twenty third Day of September in the yeare of our Lord 1654.

Jo: Warde.

Be it remembred that John Thornton and Mary Huby both of the Parish of Monkfriston hath come before me John Ward of Tanshill Esquire and were married According to the Act in that Case made upon the Seventh Day of October In the yeare of our Lord 1654.

Jo: Warde.

Be it Remembred that Robart Hemingway and Elizabeth Northin both of the pish of Monckfriston hath come before John Ward of Tanshill Esquire and were married According to the Act in that Case made upon the ffourth Day of November In the yeare of our Lord 1654.

Jo: Warde.

Be it Remembred that William Wilson of Bigging in the pish of ffenton and Jane Berrie of the pish of Monckfriston hath come before me John Odingsels of Reast Parke in the County of York one of the Justices of peace for the West Riding and were married according to the Act in that case made the last Day of November 1654.

Jo: Odingsels.

Be it remembred that Thomas Clarke and Marie Collett both of the pish of Monk-friston hath come before me John Ward of Tanchill in the County of Yorke Esquire one of the Justices of the peace for the West Ridinge & were married accordinge to the Act in that case made the thirteenth day of Januarij 1654.

Jo: Warde.

Be it Remembred that George Illingworth of Hillam in the pish of Monckfriston And Grace Nickson of Barstow in the pish of Sherburne hath come before me John Ward of Tanchill in the County of York Esquire one of the Justices of the peace for the West Riddinge and were married accordinge to the Act in that Case made the 24th of March 1654

Jo: Warde.

Be it remembred that Charles Smyth & Alice Dobsone both of the pish of Monck-friston hath come before me John Warde of Tanchill in the County of York Esq one of the Justices of the West Ridinge & were married Accordinge to the Act in that case made the thirteenth Day of July In the yeare of our Lord 1655.

Jo: Warde.

Be it Rememberd that Bartholomewe Hollingworth of the pish of Shereburne And Mabell Toppin of Burton Salmon in the pish of Monckfriston hath come before me John Warde of Tanchill in the County of Yorke Esquire one of the Justices of the peace for the West ridinge And were married Accordinge to the Act in that Case made the third day of Nouember 1655.

                                                    Jo: Warde.

Be it Remembred that Christoper Lee of Burton Salmon in the pish of Monck-friston And Marie ffostard of the same parish hath come before me John Warde of Tanchill in the County of Yorke Esquire one of the Justices of the peace for the West Riddinge And were married According to the Act in that case made the ffifteenth day of December in the yeare of our Lord 1655.

                                                    Jo: Warde.

Be it Remembred that William Batman of the pish of Ledsham And Margarett Todd of the pish of Monckfriston hath come before me John Ward of Tanchill in the County of Yorke Esquire And were married Accordinge to the Act in that case made the twenty nynth day of March in the yeare of our Lord 1656.

                                                    Jo: Warde.

Be it Remembred that John Gylsone And Jane Hemingway both of the pish of Monkfriston hath come before Mr John Warde of Tanshelfe in the County of Yorke Esquire And were married Accordinge to the Act in that case made the sixt Day of May in the yeare of our Lord 1656.

                                                    Jo: Warde.

Be it Remembred that William Hollend of Susworth in the pish of Scotton in the County Lincoln & Anne Spinke of Burton in the pish of Monckfriston hath come before me John Ward of Tanshelfe in the County of Yorke Esquire And were married the seaventeenth Day of July in the yeare of our Lord 1656.

                                                    Jo: Warde.

Be it Remembred that William Rimmington of Gatefforth in the pish of Braton & Anne Spinke of Hillam in the pish of Monckfriston hath come before me John Ward of Tanchelfe in the County of Yorke Esquire And were married the second day of August In the yeare of our Lord 1656.

                                                    Jo: Warde.

Be it Remembred that Ralph Taylor of Burton Salmon in the parish of Monck-friston & Anne Craven of the pish of Saxton hath come before mee Mathew ffranke of Pontefract in the County of Yorke Esqr And were married the thirteenth day of October in the yeare of our Lord 1656.

                                                    Ma: ffranck.

Be it Remembred that Samuell Jenkinsone And Anne Bramham both in the pish of Monckfriston hath come before mee John Ward of Tanchelfe in the County of York Esquire one of the Justices of the peace for the West riding And were married the sixteenth day of May 1657.

Be it Remembred that Thomas Tarboton & Issabell Nelson both of the pish of Monckfriston hath come before me Mathew ffrancke of Pontefract in the County of Yorke Esquire one of the justices of the peace for the West riddinge and were married the twenty third day of May in the yeare of our Lord 1657.

Be it known & remembred that all these marriages were &c.

1654.

Bir : Marmaduke sonne of John Stamford borne July 17th.

September.

B.	George sonne of Thomas Gamble borne	3d
Bur.	Anne wife of John Berry buryed	12
B.	Elizabeth doughter of Thamos Richardson borne.	
Bur.	Sarah daughter of John Berry buryed	Oct. 14
B.	Robert sonne of James Webster borne	Nov. 1
B.	Jane daughter of John West borne	Nov. 7
B.	Dorothy daughter of Richard Roundall borne	December 2
Bur.	Margret Nutter buryed	18
B.	Mary daughter of Edward Procter borne	decem. 19
Bur.	Margaret wife of Will'm Shaw buryed	January 9th
B.	Richard sonne of Thomas Harrison borne	28
Bur.	Elizabeth daughter of Anne Nelson buryed	ffebruary 4th
B.	Alice daughter of Anthony Heptonstall borne	8th
B.	Margret daughter of Luke Middleton borne	9
B.	Rosamond daughter of John Bingley borne	14
B.	Will'm sonne of Andrew Armestrong borne	28
Bur.	Marmaduke sonne of Mr John Stamford buryed	March 2

1655.

Bur.	Mary ye wife of Mr Marmaduke Blakiston buryed	April 11th
B.	Harebred sonne of Mr Thomas Norman borne	12
Bur.	George Tutill buryed	15
Bur.	Rob't Wright buryed	17
B.	Alice daughter of Robert Cockill Borne	22
B.	Timothy sonne of Timothy Bramham borne	26
Bur.	Elizabeth daughter of Mr Marmaduke Blakiston buryed	May 4
B.	John sonne of John Spinke borne	24
B.	Roger sonne of George Bew Junior borne	June 11
B.	Will'm sonne of Henry Dixon borne	24
Bur.	Will'm sonne of Henry Dixon buryed July	10
B.	John sonne of George Browne borne the	15
B.	Anne daughter of Rob't Harrison borne	18
Bur.	A Crizam childe of Anne Taylors buryed	20
Bur.	Anne Taylor widdow buryed	22
B.	Richard sonne of Rob't Hemmingway borne August	2
Bur.	Richard Whiteheade a swine driver of Wakefeild who dyed on ye Cawsey	} buryed 25.
Bur.	Elizabeth daughter of Marmaduke Gilliam borne	.. 9
B.	Jane daughter of William Hemmingway borne	10
B.	Mary daughter of Arthur Topcliffe borne September	8
Bur.	Mary daughter of George Bew Buryed Octob:	15
B.	Mary dau. of Ellis Halliley borne November	29
Bur.	Anne who dwelt at Abraham Taylers buryed Dec.	9
B.	Bryan sonne of Luke Danyel borne January	8
B.	Elizabeth Wilson daughter of Wilson Wilson borne	9
Bur.	Anne Procter widdow buryed	10
B.	Jane daughter of Thomas Dickon borne	12
B.	Margret daughter of Mr John Tomlinson borne	13
Bur.	Elizabeth Graves buryed	16
B.	Will'm sonne of Michael Cowling borne	ffeb. 15
B.	Edward sonne of Thomas Robinson borne	24
B.	ffrances daughter of Mr Matthew Hall borne	

14

Bur. a Crizam childe of John bustard buryed March	21
B. Will'm sonne of John Nelson borne	22
Bur. Robt Halliley buryed	22
B. Thomas sonne of Thomas Robinson borne	27

1656.

Bur. Henry Dixon buryed	31
Bur. Edward Hemingway buryed Aprill	2
B. . . . . daughter of Will'm Biskom borne	4
B. Thomas Richardson buryed	8
Bur. Mr John Wilson buryed	9
B. Will'm sonne of ffrancis Waude borne	16
Bur. Jan Harrison buryed	21
Bur. Richard sonne of Luke Middleton buryed May ·	2
B. Henry sonne of Henry dixon deceased borne	2
Bur. Will'm Cleane buryed	4
Bur. Timothy sonne of Timothy Bramham buryed	13
Bur. Henry sonne of Henry dixon buryed	15
Bur. Margret daughter of Mr John Tomlinson buryed	17
B. Anne daughter of Mr John Stamforth borne	17
Bur. . . . . wife of James Naylor buryed	30
Bur. Margret daughter of Mr John Wilson deceased buryed June	2
Bur. Phillip Camage buryed July	27
B. Crizam Childe of Thomas Clarkes buried August	4 day
B. Elezabeth wife of Richard Hemingway buried the	15 day
C. Thomas sone of Edward Walker borne the	15 day

                             September vacat.

October.

B. Will'm Swifte buried the	7 day

November.

B. Alce wife of John Lee buried the	18 day
B. Anne wife of Richard Northing buried the	29 day

december.

B. Anne wife of Edward Lunde buried the	3 day
C. Will'm sone Will'm Batman borne the 3 day.	
B. A Crizam Childe of John Pearsons buried the 6 day.	
C. Anne Daughter of Andrew Armestrong borne the 24 day.	

Januarie.

B. Anne Daughter of Andrew Armestronge buried the 20 day.

B. Godfray Spinke buried the	22 day
B. Margrit Bramham buried the	30 day

ffebruarie.

B. Elizabeth Daughter of Will'm Willson buried 2 day.
B. James Bedforth buried the 5 day.
C. Margret Daughter of John Gyllson borne the 15 day.
C. John sonne of John Letham of milford borne the 16 day.

March.

C. Elizabeth Daughter of Richard Smith of milford borne 2.
C. Alce daughter of Xpofer Lee borne the 3 day.
C. Thomas sonne of Mr Thomas Norman borne the 15 day.

Aprill 1657.

B. Will'm Atkinson buried the 7th day.
C. Anne Daughter of John Barker the 10 day.
B. Richard Lumax buried the 15 day.

May.

B. Dorathe Swifte buried the 3 day.
B. John sonne of Thomas Leatham buried the 19 day.
B. George sonne of Will'm Shaw buried the 19 day.
B. A Crizam Childe of George Ellingworth buried the 29 day.
C. John sonne of George Ellingworth borne the 29 day.

June vacat.

July.

B. Grace Crosland buried the   12 day.
B. Anne Spinke wife of Thomas Spinke tanner buried 13 day.

August.

B. ffrancis Daughter of Mr Mathew Hall buried the first day.
B. Jane wife of Robert Clarke buried the 7 day.
B. Will'm Atkinson buried the 17 day.
B. Jennit Hamond widow buried the 19 day.
B. Margret wife of Will'm Smith buried the 22 day.

September.

B. Margret daughter of George Harbott buried the 4 day.
B. George Gylliam buried the 5 day.
B. Thomas Robinsone buried the 10 day.
C. Hellinge Daughter of Thomas Harrison borne the 21 day.
C. Will'm sonne of Arther Hamond borne the 30 day.

October.

B. Richard Northin buried the first day.
C. John sonne of John Tayler borne the 6 day.
B. John Swifte buried the 8 day.
B. Katheren wife of Abraham Taler buried the 10 day.
B. Will'm sonne of Arther Hawmand buried the 18 day.
B. Elizabeth Cleane widdow buried the 19 day.
B. Will'm Mason buried the 20 day.
B. Dorathe Durnill widdow buried the 20 day.

Nouember.

C. Thomas sonne of Thomas Richardson of Yorke borne the 3 day.
C. Omphray sonne of John Spinke borne the 6 day.
B. Elizabeth Bustard widdow buried the 12 day.
B. Alce Lumbie widdow buried the 15 day.
B. A Crizam Childe of Thomas Clarkes borne & buried the 20 day.
B. Robert Clarke buried the 30 day.

December.

B. Mr Marmaduke Blackston buried the 14 day.
B. Edward Prockter buried the 15 day.
B. Robert Berridge buried the 18 day.
B. Marie Harrison buried the 24 day.

december 1657.

B. John Leatham buried the 24 day.
B. Elezabeth Lumax buried the 27 day.
B. Jane wife of John Gyllson buried the 29 day.

Januarie.

B. Alce daughter of George Hemingway buried the 14 day.
B. Robert Craven the yonger buried the 25 day.
C. ffrancis Daughter of M' Mathew Hall borne the 26 day.
B. ffrancis Nelson buried the 28 day.

ffebruarie.

B. Robert Cockell buried the first day.
B. Jane wife of Richard Stubes buried the second day.
B. Henerie Turpin buried the 23 day.
B. Will'm Hartlay buried the 24 day.

March.

B. Thomas Leatham buried the 10 day.
C. John sonne of Ralph Tayler borne the 16 day.
B. Will'm Penrose buried the 24 day.

Aprill 1658.

M. Robert Berridge & Dorathe flockton married the 13 day.
B. Tymithe Bramham buried the 15 day.
C. Anne Daughter of M' Richard Atkinson borne the 16 day.
B. George Welles buried the 20 day.
C. Mathew sonne of Thomas Beadshay baptized the 27 day.

May.

C. Sarah Daughter of George Bew Junier baptized 10 day.
C. Robert Sonne of Robert Cockell baptized the 18 day.
M. James Robinson & Alce Cartwright married the 26 day.
                                    June vacat.

July.

C. Elezabeth daughter of Richard Hemingway Junier bap^t 14^d.

August.

B. M^{tris} Marie Atkinsone wife of Mr Richard Atkinson died at Monckfrieston the
       15 & buried at Boltan Poirrie the 16^d.
M. Abraham Tayler & Elizabeth Barber married the 19 day

September.

C. Robert Harrisan son of Robert Harrisan bapt the 5 day.
B. John sonne of George Illingworth buried the 10 day.
M. Mathew Lunde & Jane Ledsam married the 22 day.
B. Robert Harrisan of Hillam buried the 25 day.
C. Marie Daughter of Mr Richard Sikes esquire baptiz the 30 day.

October.

B. Marie Daughter of Arther Topliffe buried the 2 day.
C. Timethe sonne of mabell Bramham bap^{tis} 14 day.

October Anno Dom. 1658.

B. Anthonie Summers buried the 17 day.
C. Henerie sonne of Ralph ffeatan baptiz 17 day.
B. Alce Atkinson widow buried the 19 day.
C. .... Daughter of James Webster baptized the 24 day.
B. Marie wife of Joseph Nelsan buried the 25 day.
B. Anne wife of James Webster buried the 27 day.

Nouember.

B. ffrancis wife of Richard Hall buried the 3 day.
M. Will'm Smith & Margret Shaw married the 18 day.
B. Elizabeth Daughter of Charles Smith buried the 23 day.

December.

B. Elizabeth daughter of Richard Hemingway buried the firste day.
B. Elezabeth Summers widdow buried the 5 day.
B. Anne wife of Robert fforth buried the 12 day.
B. A Crizam childe of Edward Walkers buried the 13 day.
B. Thomas Spinke of Hillam buried the 14 day.
B. Anthonie Hepenstall of meltan Leyes buried 14 day.
B. John son of Ralph Tayler buried the 15 day.
C. Elezabeth Daughter of Mr Grantham Langley bap{t} the 26 day.
C. Mathew sonne of Bartholomew Hollingworth bapt the 26 day.
B. Anne Daughter of widdow Rickinson of Hillam buried ye 27d.

Januarie.

B. Thomas Tutill of Burton buried the 3 day.
B. Thomas Tayler of Hillam buried the 4 d.

ffebruarie.

B. Martha Daughter of Peter Blanchard baptiz: the 24.

March.

B. Richard sonne of Andrew Armestronge baptiz the 6 day.
B. Robert ffirth of Barton buried the 16 day.
C. Anne Daughter of Henery Stillinge baptized the 17 day.

Aprill 1659.

B. Elezabeth Hallelay Widdow buried the first day.
C. Marie Daughter of John Taler baptized the 3 day.
C. .... of Thomas Terbison baptized the 5 day.
C. Marie Daughter of George Illingworth baptized 9 day.
B. Anne Spinke widdow buried 15 day.
B. Robert Walker of Hillam buried the 17 day.
B. Elizabeth Daughter of John Berrie buried the 26 day.

June.

C. Elizabeth Doughter of Arther Topliffe baptized the 12 day.
C. Anne Daughter of Mr Thomas Norman baptized 21 day.
B. Elling sawer widdow buried 22 day.

July.

B. Elezabeth Dawsan widdow buried at Ledsam the 23 day.

Anno Dom. 1659.

M. Joseph Nelsan & Annie Hurst married the 28 day.
M. James Webster & Helling Skelton married the 28 day.

September.

C. Robert sonne of Robert Berridge baptized the first day.
B. Anne the wife of James Rawsan the 4 day.

October.

B. Anne the Daguhter of Mr Richard Atkinson buried the 20 day.
C. John the sonne of William Batman baptized the 23 day.
C· Abraham the sonne of Abraham Tayler baptized the 27 day.
B. John sonne Will'm Batman buried the 30 day.

Nouember.

B. Jane wife of Robert Hemingway of Hillam buried 7 d.
C. Francis the sone of Francis Waude baptized the 24 d.
M. Bartholamew Hepenstall & Izabell Willson married December.

December.

C. Will'm sonne of Joseph Nelson baptized the 22 day.
B. Richard Stubbes buried the 14 day of Januarie
M. John Johnsan & mabel Bramham marryed the 18 day of Januarie.

Januarie.

B. John Tod buried the xx day.
B. Anne Mason widdow buried xxij day.

ffebruarie Anno Regis Caroli 2di 12º.

B. Marie Daughter of Edward Prockter buried the xij day.
C. Thomas sonne of John Nelsan baptized xiix day.
C. Margret Daughter of George Harbott baptized xxj day.

March.

M. Edward Lunde & Elizabeth Shan married the x day.
M. Henrie Splayforth & Elizabeth Robinson married xij day.
C. Christopher sonne of Posthumus Spinke baptized xxv day.
C. Marie Daughter of John Hutton baptized the xxvj day.

Aprill 1660 *Anno Regis Caroli secundi* 12.

M. Robert Steedman of ·Shearburne & Anne Cockell Widdow of this towne
    married the iij day.
B. Elizabeth Barber of Hillam widdow buried iiij day.
B. Anne ffaburne widdow buried the xiij day.
C. Richard sonne of Mr Richard Sykes Esquire baptized the xxv day.
B. Richard sonne of Thomas Harrisan buried xxvj day.
C. Will'm sonne of Will'm Smyth baptiz the xxix day.
B. John Berrie pish Clarke buried the xxx day.

May.

Richard Hemingway Chozen pish Clarke the viij day.
C. Charels sonne of Marmaduke Gyllyam baptz thee xvij day.
B. Will'm sonne of ffrancis Waude buried the xviij day.

Robert Harrisan buried the xx day.
Christopher sonne of posthumus Spinke buried xxvij day.

Ano Dom 1660 Regis Caroli 2di 12o.

June.

Margret Daughter of George Harbot buried the iij.
Anne the wife of Nicolas Wailles buried the viij.
Thomas sonne of John Nelson buried the xv day.

September.

Godfrey sonne of Bartholamew Hollingworth of milforth bap x.
Marie Daughter of Henery Splayforth baptized xx day.
John Sonne of John Gilson baptized the xxj day.
Elizabeth Daughter of James Webster baptized xxiij day.

October.

Elizabeth Daughter of Will'm Biskam baptiz ⎫
Marthay Daughter of Mathew Lunde baptiz ⎬ the first.
Edward Sonne of Richard Hemingway baptiz ⎭
Elezabeth Daughter of Edward Lunde baptized xiij day.

Nouember.

Will'm Willson & Jane Dickson married the xvj day.
Anne the Daughter of John Spinke baptiz the xviij day.

December.

Elizabeth Daughter of John Busterd baptized the xvij day.
Januarie vacat.

ffebruarie Anno Caroli 2di 13.

Robert sonne of Edward Walker baptiz xv day.

March.

Marie daughter of Mr Thomas Norman baptized xj day.
Will'm sonne of Robert Hemmingway baptized xviij day.
Marie Daughter of Robert Hemingway baptized xx day.
John sonne of Will'm Wilson baptiz xx day.

Aprill 1661. Anno Regis Caroli Secundi 13.

Mr Edward Chatterton buried the xx day.
Edward sonne of John Tayler baptized the xx day.
Elizabeth Daughter of John Bustard buried the xxviij day.
John the sonne of Will'm Willson buried the xxix day.
Izabell Daughter of Anthonie Hepenstall baptiz xxx day.

May.

Anne the Daughter of Henerie Stillinge buried the xvij day.
Joseph the sonne of John ffabarne baptized the ⎫ xix.
Elizabeth Daughter of Posthumus Spinke baptized the ⎭

June.

John Nickson & Elezabeth Richardson maried iij day.
ffrances Daughter of John Binglay of Lumbie baptized iiij day.
Edward the sonne of John Tayler buried the vj day.
Thomas the sonne of Richard Roundell baptized the xij day.
Margret the Daughter of Will'm Ashton xvij.

July Anno Domini 1661 *Caroli* 2^{di} 13.

B.   Edward son of Thomas Robinson buried viij.

August.

B.   Joseph son of John ffaburne buried iij.
B.   Elizabeth Daughter of Will'm Bispam buried v.
B.   Anne the wife of Will'm Bispam buried vij.
B.   Will'm Shaw buried the xxx.

September.

C.   Anne the Daughter of Arther Hammand baptized viij.
B.   John Nickson buried viij.
C.   Anne the Daughter of Robert Birridge xxvij.

October.

C.   James the sonne of Hennerie Stillinge baptized iiij.
C.   Thomas the sonne of George Bew baptized v.
B.   ffrancis Waude buried the x.
C.   Michell sonne of Joseph Nellsan baptized xij.
C.   Anne Daughter of George Ilingworth xij.
B.   Grace the wife of George Ilingworth xviij.
B.   Mr Tobias Swinden prebent of the p'bendarie (prebendary of the p'bend)
      Wistow xxv.

December.

Ellinge Daughter of John Nellsan baptized viij.
dorithy Daughter of Robert Welles baptized xxvj.
Mabell wife of John Johnson buried the same day.
Thomas sonne of Thomas Beardshey Januarie the v.

Januarie.

Marie the wife of Edward Clarke buried xviij.
Anne Carbie widdow buried the xx
Will'm Sonne of Arther Topliffe baptized xxvj.

ffebruarie Anno Regis Caroli 2^{di} 14.

Margret the wife of Marke Andertan buried the xvj.
Bridgite Daughter of Elezabeth Leatham buried the xvij.
Thomas Raine buried xxij.
John Graye buried xxiij.
Will'm the sonne of Robert Hemingway buried xxvij.
A Crizam Childe of Richard Gillyam buried xxviij.

March.

C.   Anne the Daughter of Richard Sturdie baptized ij.
B.   Will'm the sonne of Thomas Hartlay buried vj.

Anno doni 1662 : regis Car : Secund 14.

Aprill   { W : Strode came to Monkfriston Apr. 5
                { 1662 : Œtatis 23.
M.   Adam Harrisan and Elizabeth Gyllsan married xxix.

May.

B.   Anne the Daughter of John Spinke buried j.
M.   James Bramham and Marie Hemingway married xxviij
C.   John sonne of John Bustard baptized xxix.

June.

. Ann the daughter of Thomas Tarbetan baptized xj.
. Thomas son of Thomas Beardshay buried the same day.
. Mary the daughter of Robert Hemingway buried 13.

July.

. Thomas son of Peter Bell baptized 13.
. M\ Elizabeth Hammond buried 16.
. Thomas son of John Tayler baptized 20.

August.

. James son of William Smith baptized 3.
l. John Johnson & Elizabeth Leatham married 7.
. Robert son of Francis Waud baptized the same day.
. Ann daughter of William Wilson of Hilham baptized 10.
. Thomas son of John Taylor buried 16.
. William son of William Sawer buried 24.
. Mary daughter of Richard Heptenstall bap 31.
. and buried the same day.

September.

. Mary daughter of Thomas Brown of Burton bap\ 14.

September Anno dni 1662 Caroli 2di.

l. William Wilkinson & Ann Roundall married.

October.

. Francis Clerke son of Edward Clerk buried 1.
. John son of John Wells baptized 12.

Novembr

. Alice daughter of Henry Splayforth baptized   12
l. Rob\ Fox & Margaret Settle married   13
. Alice daughter of Henry Splayforth buried   20
. Ann Rawson widdow buried   27
. Thomas son of Thomas Routh baptized   30

December.

. Ann the wife of George Illingworth buried   11
. Francis son of M\ Christoph\ Hammond baptized   23

January.

. An unbaptized child of Will Waud buried   2
l. Edward Swift & Mary Bramham married   27

February Anno Regis Caroli 2di 150.

. Isabell wife of Bartholomew Heppingstall buried   1
. George son of M\ Thomas Norman baptized   2
. Robert son of Robert Empson buried   5
. Timothy son of Timothy Bramham buried   15
. George son of Lancelot Bew baptized   24
. Ursula wife of Roger Northing buried   27

15

March.

M.	George Twisleton & Elizabeth Clerke married	2
C.	Ann the daughter of John Spink baptized	15
B.	Jane wife of Will'm Barwick buried	17
B.	.... son of Thomas Huddleston buried	21
C.	Francis son of John Johnson baptized	22
C.	Mary daughter of James Bramham baptized	29

Apr. Aº d'ni 1663.

	William son of Will'm Gilson of Burton baptized	17

Anno Domi May 1663 Caroli 2di 15º.

C.	Elzab daughter of William Wilkinson baptized	3
B.	Ann daughter of George Illingworth buried	7

June.

B.	Margaret Cocker widow buried	15

July.

B.	Ann Gilson wife of Will Gilson buried	8

August.

B.	Francis son of John Johnson buried	8
C.	John son of Thomas Hodgson baptized	9
B.	Ann Spink widow of Burton buried	13
C.	Mary daughter of George Gilson baptized	20

September.

B.	A child of Marmaduke Guilliam buried	6
C.	Frances daughter of John Hoiland baptized	10
B.	Marmaduke Guilliam buried	14
B.	Elizabeth daughter of Edward Walker buried	16
B.	Dorothy wife of Richard Guilliam buried	19
B.	Agnes Tailor widow buried	21

October.

M.	Mark Anderton & Elizabeth Brook married	1
C.	John son of Thomas Bearshey baptized	11
M.	Will Biskam & Elizabeth Procter married	22
B.	William son of John Nelson buried	14
B.	Jennet wife of Richard Ryly of Milford buried	28
B.	John son of Joseph Nelson buried	30

November.

B.	Frances wife of Henry Green buried	1
C.	Ann daughter of John Tailor baptized	8

December.

C.	William son of Abraham Tailor baptized	13
	buried	19

W. Strode.

December Aº dom 1663 Caroli 2di 15.

C.	Richard son of Richard Heptenstall [corrected in Register from Heppengstall] baptized	28
B.	Mr Wm Lawther buried	29

January.

B.	Joshuah son of Joseph Nelson baptized	3
M.	Wᵐ Barwick & Eliz. Brasia married ⎫	26
M.	George Atkinson & Jane Wells married ⎭	
B.	Dorothy daughter of Robt Spink baptized ⎫	31
B.	Mʳ Geo: Morret buried ⎭	

February Anno Regis Caroli secundi 16°.

C.	Jane daughter of Richard Hemingway baptized	10
C.	Robert son of Posthumus Spink baptized	28

March.

B.	Mary wife of Thomas Roundall buried	6
C.	Elizabeth daughter of Robert Empson baptized	29

April 1664.

B.	Widow Foister buried	5
C.	Esther daughter of Mathew Berkinshey baptized	17
C.	William son of Rob't Berridge baptized	19
C.	James son of Thomas Rawson baptized	26

May.

B.	Eliz daughter of Eliz Harbottle buried	1
M.	Thomas Spink & Jane Bywater married	10
M.	George Illingworth & Ann Smith married	12
C.	Rob't son of William Biskam baptized	22
C.	Bartholemew son of Barthol: Heptenstall baptized	31

June.

C.	Joseph son of Thomas Liegh baptized	5
C.	George son of Geo: Bew junʳ baptized	29

July.

C.	Ann daughter of Rob't Wells baptized	3
C.	Elizabeth daughter of John Johnson baptized ⎫	24
B.	Beatrix Harrison widow buried ⎭	
M.	George Rogers & Mary Walker married	26

August.

B.	George son of George Bew junʳ buried	15
	W. Strode, Minister.	

Anno Dom. 1664. Regis Caroli Secundi 16.

August.

M.	Mʳ John Beale & Mⁿˢ Frances Lowther married	27

September.

B.	. . . . daughter of Wᵐ Richardson buried	17
C.	Elizabeth daughter of Wᵐ Berwick baptized ⎫	25
C.	Tobias son of Peter Blanchard baptized ⎭	

October.

C.	William son of Arthur Hamond baptized	9
C.	Ann Heptenstall daughter of Anthony Heptenstall ⎫ baptized	20
B.	⎭ buried	21

B. Margaret wife of Anthony Heptenstall buried ... 21
B. Jennet wife of William Bramham buried ... 30

November.

C. William son of Richard Roundall baptized ... 3
B. Thomas Gibson (? Gilson) buried ... 18
M. Wᵐ Carver & Elizabeth Nickson married ... 24

December.

B. Wᵐ son of Arthur Hamond buried ... 18

January.

C. Elizabeth daughter of John Bustard baptized ... 19

February Anno Caroli 2ᵈⁱ 17.

C. William son of John Spink baptized ... 2
C. Elizabeth daughter of Lancelot Bew baptized ... 19
C. Mary daughter of Thomas Tarbotan baptized ... 26

March.

C. Robert son of William Wilkinson baptized ... 12
C. Christopher son of Mʳ Christopher Hamond baptized ... 23
B. Robert son of William Wilkinson buried ... 26
C. John son of Marmaduke Hodgson baptized ... 28

April 1665.

C. John son of Arthur Topliff baptized ... 2
C. James son of John Gilson junior baptized ... 23

May.

C. William son of John Ingland baptized ... 9
B. .... daughter of Edward Lund Buried ... 12
M. Rob't Spink and Frances Wharton married ... 16
B. Elizabeth Grant widow buried ... 14
B. Thomas Foster buried ... 15

Aug.

C. Ann daughter of Abraham Tailour baptized ... 6
C. Elizabeth daughter of Mʳ John Beale baptized ... 9
C. Edward son of Henry Splayforth baptized ... 20
B. Noell son of Grantham Langly buried ... 24
B. Mʳˢ Norman buried ... 26
C. Ann daughter of Wᵐ Richardson baptized ... 27

Anno Dni. 1665. September Anno Caroli 2ᵈⁱ 17.

B. William son of John Spink buried ... 3
B. William son of Mʳ Richard Sikes buried ... 23

October.

C. Mathew son of Mathew Lund baptized ... 10
B. John Pereson buried ... 19

November.

M. Robert Thwait (?) & Elizabeth Thwart (?) married ⎱ 14
C. Elizabeth daughter of Hugh Revell baptized ⎰
M. Richard Gwilliam and Mʳˢ Sarah Brooks married ... 14
M. Matthew Pottage & Mary Jackson married ... 16

February.

Anno Caroli secundi 18.

C.	Rob't son of William Sawer baptized	3
C.	Sarah daughter of John Hoiland baptized	15

March.

C.	George son of Peter Bell baptized	11
B.	Margaret Huby buried	16

April Anno Dni 1666.

C.	Thomas son of John Tailour baptized	16
B.	Mary Meuse wife of Nicholas Meuse buried	28

May.

C.	Mary daughter of tho: Tinker baptized	6
M.	Thomas Tofield (?) & Jane Thwait married	8

June.

B.	Mary Turner daughter of Richard Turner buried	
C.	Thomas son of Rob't Spink baptized	5
B.	A child still born of Geo: Atkinson buried	6
B.	James son of Wᵐ Smith buried	12
B.	Richard Hemingway junʳ Parish Clerk buried	16

July.

C.	Elizabeth daughter of Rob't Spink senʳ baptized	3

August.

C.	Elizabeth daughter of Edward Walker ⎫ baptized	5
C.	Jane daughter of John Spink ⎬	
B.	Elizabeth daughter of Hugh Revell buried	5
C.	Mary daughter of Thomas Beardshey baptized	12

September.

M.	Edward Hodgson & Elizabeth Guilliam married.
C.	Ann daughter of John Nelson baptized.
B.	Elizabeth Tod buried.

W. Strode.

B.	Ann daughter of John Nelson buried	23
B.	Edward Hodgson buried	24
B.	Isabel Nelson wife of John Nelson buried	25
C.	John son of Richard Heptenstall baptized	26

October.

C.	Richard son of Richard Guilliam baptized ⎫	
B.	.... daughter of John Hoiland buried ⎬ 7	
B.	Ellen wife of John Laverack buried ⎭	
C.	Alice daughter of Rob't Berridge baptized	9
B.	James son of Wᵐ Smith buried	17
C.	Thomas son of Thomas Rawson baptized	24
C.	John son of Matthew Berkinshey baptized	28

November.

C.	Susanna daughter of Wᵐ Wilkinson baptized	4
B.	.... son of Richard Ward buried	14

December.

B.	Rob't Hemingway buried	4
C.	Ann daughter of James Bramham baptized	6
C.	Ann Posthumous daughter of Richard Hemingway baptized	11
C.	Ann daughter of John Bustard baptized	20
B.	Charles Smith buried	29

January.

B.	Mary Wells buried	4
B.	John Wells buried	10
C.	Stephen son of Tho: Hodgson baptized	13
C.	Ann doughter of John Erby baptized	13
B.	Jane Hemingway widow buried	31

February Anno Caroli 2di 19

B.	Rob't Craven buried	10
C.	Elizabeth daughter of Thomas Meuse	14
M.	George Wells & Jane Swift married	18

March.

B.	.... son of Thomas Hodgson buried	2
C.	Jane daughter of John Gilson baptized	10

Aprill Anno Dni 1667.

B.	William Nelson buried	6
M.	W. Gilson & Grace Swift married	11
B.	Elizabeth wife of Arthur Topliff buried	12

Anno Dni 1667 Caroli 2di 19.

April.

B.	Matthew Lund buried	28

May.

C.	Mary daughter of Hugh Revell baptized	1
C.	Ann daughter of Wm Berwick baptized	
B.	.... son of Matthew Lund buried	5

May.

M.	Arthur Topcliff & .... married	28

June.

B.	Ann wife of George Bew junr buried	13
B.	Ann wife of John Faburn buried	19
B.	Wm Bocock buried	20
C.	John son of Wm Gilson junior baptized	30

July.

B.	Elizabeth wife of John Johnson buried	18
B.	Gervase son of Geo: Illingworth baptized	21
B.	Thomas Clark buried	23
B.	John son of John Hoiland baptized	29

August.

B.	Wm Lowther buried	8
B.	John son of John Hoiland buried	

Charles son of Ann Guilliam buried	17
Margaret daughter of Joseph Nelson baptized	18

September.

William son of .... Wells baptized	1
Sarah daughter of Mr Christopher Hamond baptized	3

October.

John son of Geo: Laverack baptized	3
Elizabeth Leper buried	11

November.

Wm Overton buried	1
Susan daughter of John Cockill buried	8
Alice daughter of Lancelot Bew baptized	10

December.

Ann daughter of Geo: Wells baptized	2
Matthias son of Rob't Spink baptized	5
Mary daughter of John Ingland baptized	7
& buried	8

Anno Domini. 1667 Caroli Secundi 19.

December.

Martin son of John Tailour baptized	8
Mrs Frances Beale buried	27

January.

Jane daughter of Wm Richardson baptized	
Rob't son of Geo: Atkinson baptized	1
Mary Illingworth buried	
James son of Wm Smith baptized	5
Arthur Hammond buried	11
Elizabeth daughter of Mr John Beale buried	19

Anno Caroli 2^{di} 20. Anno D^{no} 166⅞.

February.

W^m son of Thomas Hodgson baptized	16
Rob't Turner buried	20

March.

W^m son of John Cutt baptized	5
.... daughter of John Gilson jun^r buried	19
Henry Green buried Easter day	22

Aprill Anno Domini 1668.

John Musgrave & Ann Wells married	30

June.

Elizabeth daughter of Thomas Meuse buried	6
Thomas son of John Faburn baptized	28

July.

Jane wife of Geo: Spink buried	7
John Ingland buried	14
.... daughter of Arthur Topliff buried	24

August.

B.	Isabel wife of Hugh Revell buried	10
B.	Widow Foster buried	16
C.	Thomas son of Benjamin Spink baptized	18
C.	Elizabeth daughter of James Bramham baptized }	
B.	Esther wife of James Bramham buried }	20

Anno Dni. 1668 Caroli 2nd 20.

C.	Katherine daughter of John Spink baptized	30
B.	Elizabeth daughter of James Bramham buried	31

September.

B.	William son of John Cutt buried	3
C.	Henry son of Thomas Tarbotan baptized	24

October.

B.	Roger Northing buried	17

November.

B.	Jane Proctour buried	1
C.	.... son of John Altus or Althouse	15
C.	Margaret daughter of Edward Lund	
C.	Mary daughter of John Hoiland baptized	10

December.

B.	George Spink buried	2
B.	George Bew the elder buried	27

January.

B.	.... daughter of John Gilson jun^r buried	5
B.	William Waud buried	16
B.	Thomas Spink buried	17
C.	Ann daughter of Tho: Rawson baptized	18
C.	Jane daughter of Rob't Spink baptized	21
B.	.... daughter of Joseph Nelson buried	25

Anno Caroli 21.

February.

B.	Grace Ledsham buried	7
C.	William son of Richard Heptenstall baptized	9
B.	Ann daughter of Alice Brasbrig baptized	14
B.	Richard son of Richard Heptenstall buried	18
C.	Mary daughter of John Erby baptized	21

March.

B.	Elizabeth daughter of John Johnson buried	11
B.	.... of John Faburn buried	13
B.	.... daughter of Wm Hemingway buried	

March 1669. Anno Caroli 2di 21.

C.	Jane daughter of John Bustard baptized	25

Aprill. 1669.

C.	James son of Abraham Tailour baptized	18
C.	Thomas son of Thomas Meuse baptized	22

Thomas son of Tho: Meuse buried   23
Wm Wilson of Hillom buried   27

May.

Robert son of Wm Lund baptized   9
Frances Wright buried   13

June.

Margaret daughter of Tho Wilson baptized   1
Mr Wm Colinson & Elleno' Waud married   10
Robert son of Mr Tho: Norman baptized   21
Robert son of Mr Tho: Norman buried   22

July vacat.

August.

Anthony son of Joseph Prat Christened   2
Sarah daughter of Mr Rob't Hews baptized   12
Mary daughter of James Bramham baptized   26
Wm Hemingway buried
Ann daughter of Tho: West baptized   29
Ann daughter of Tho: West baptized

September.

John Nelson buried   10
Isabel Morrice buried   13
John son of Rob't Berridge baptized   23
           buried   24
Dorothy wife of Rob't Berridge buried   25

October.

William son of Thomas Bateson baptized   20
Michael son of Peter Bell baptized   23
Isabel wife of Peter Bell buried   24
Michael son of Peter Bell buried   26

Nov. 1669.

.... son of Robert Wells buried   10
Richard Hemingway buried   13
Wm Johnson & Ann Cockhill married   18
Mary daughter of Geo: Wells baptized   20
Ann daughter of Geo: Illingworth baptized   21
Mary daughter of Geo: Wells buried   22

December.

John son of Rob't Spink baptized   12
Sarah daughter of Marmaduke Hodgson bapt   22
Robert son of Wm Sawer buried   26

January.

Jane daughter of Lancelot Bew bapt   1
Nicholas Mewse buried   7
Mary daughter of John Hoiland buried   16
Margaret daughter of Wm Wells baptized   23

Anno Caroli secundi 22.

February.

Margaret daughter of Wm Welles buried   11
Thomas son of Benjamin Spink
Frances daughter of Wm Bewick   baptized   20

16

March.

B. Mary Turner wife of Rich: Turner buried   4
C. John son of John Cutt baptized   15

April 1670.

C. Joane daughter of Geo: Laverack baptized   1
B. Joane daughter of Geo: Laverack buried   13

May.

M. Wᵐ Bramham and Ellen Vary married   10
C. Elizabeth daughter of Geo: Gilson baptized   15
B. .... daughter of Wᵐ Richardson buried

June.

C. Ruth daughter of Benjamin Spink baptized   1
C. Bridget daughter of Wᵐ Biskam baptized
M. John Flint & Elizabeth Bramham married   13
C. Mary daughter of Mʳ Hamond baptᵗ   14
C. Thomas son of Tho: Meuse baptᵗ   23

July.

M. John Chambers & Eliz. Saner (? Sawer) married   7

August.

B. John Spink buried   }
C. Alice daughter of Wᵐ Johnson baptized   }   29

September.

B. Francis Pitts of Hemsworth buried   4
B. Mary Harrison buried   5
B. .... daughter of Geo: Gilson buried   6
B. .... daughter of Rob't Spink buried   10
B. William Smith buried   24
B. .... wife of Wᵐ Berwick buried   25

October.

B. John Illingworth buried   5
M. Thomas Johnson & Eliz. Wilson married   6
B. Robert Wells buried   9
B. .... wife of Geo: Atkinson buried   }
C. Mary daughter of Geo: Atkinson baptized }   17
B. Luke Midleton buried   19
B. Ann wife of John Tailour buried   20
B. Jane daughter of Lancelot Bew buried   30
B. Mary daughter of John Tailour buried   31

November.

M. Peter Bell & Ann Bew married   3
C. John son of James Easingwood of Milford baptized }
C. Elizabeth daughter of Wᵐ Richardson baptized   }   13

W. Strode.

November 1670.

B. Mʳ Thomas Norman buried   23
C. Richard son of Wᵐ Wilkinson baptized   26

December.

Ann daughter of Wm Ward baptized	1
William Lund buried	4
Edward Lund buried	5
Alice Bew buried	6
Elizabeth Posthumous daughter of John Spink baptized	15
Anthony son of Joseph Prat baptized	17
[This entry has been erased in the Register.]	
Mary daughter of Thomas Liegh bap^t	18
William son of John Wood baptized	23

January.

Richard son of Wm Wilkinson buried	2
William son of John Wood buried	14
William son of John Althouse baptized	22

February.

William son of John Althouse buried	22
Elizabeth Hemingway buried	eod.

March.

Geo. Bew & Elizabeth Lund married	6
. . . . wife of Edward Walker buried	7
. . . . wife of Robert Berridge buried	18

Aprill 1671.

W^m son of William Wells baptized	16
Jane Bramham buried	
Henry Morton & Eliz. Brerecliff married	25

May.

John Leak & Jane Turner married	29

W. Strode.

Ann Bearding buried

July vacat.
August vacat.
Sep^t vacat.

October.

. . . . son of Rob't Spink buried	4

November.

James son of James Bramham baptized	5
Matthew Bolton buried	8
. . . . Cotes buried	9
Thomas son of John Bingly buried	13
ffrances wife of Thomas Ingland buried	19
James son of James Bramham of Burton baptized	26

December.

Jane daughter of Geo: Bew baptized	10
Elizabeth wife of Lancelot Bew buried	29

January.

Grace Ingland buried	25

February.

C.	Gabriell son of Benjamin Spink Xned	15
C.	James son of John Althouse Christned	20
B.	.... wife of James Butler buried	21
C.	Jane daughter of Wᵐ Ward Christned	25

March.

B.	Thomas Hodgson } buried	6
B.	John Hodgson }	

W. Strode.

March 1672.

C.	George son of Geo: Laverack Christned	10
C.	Robert son of Mʳ Rob't Hews Christned	12
C.	Elizabeth daughter of Peter Bell Christned	17

Aprill 1672.

M.	Edward Wright & Mary Guilliam married	9
B.	William Ward buried	13
C.	Jane daughter of Thomas West bapt.	21
B.	Hellen daughter of Geo: Illingworth buried	28

May.

C.	George son of Geo: Illingworth Christned	27

June.

C.	Jane daughter of John Erby Christned	13
	Ann daughter of Ellen Beatson buried	14
	Richard .... servᵗ to John Bingly buried	16

July.

	Wᵐ son of Tho: Tarbotan Christned	18

September.

C.	Mary daughter of Tho: Rawson Christned	12
B.	Elizabeth wife of Geo: Bew buried	25
B.	Widow Heptenstall buried	28

October.

C.	Joseph & Benjamin } sons of Benjamin Spink Christned	12
B.	Joseph and Benjamin } sons of Benj. Spink buried	13
B.	Thomas Rawson buried	16
B.	Matthew Berkinshey buried	31

November.

C.	Robert son of Rob't Spink Christned.

December 1672.

B.	Robert son of Rob't Spink buried.
C.	Mary daughter of John Bustard Christned.
B.	Ann Hamond buried.

February.

M. Robert Berridge & Eliz. Hodgson married.
B. Alice Cockill buried.
C. John son of George Wells Christned.
B. . . . . of . . . . Wells buried.

March.

B.	Wᵐ son of Richard Roundall buried.	
C.	William son of Geo: Gilson Christned	9
B.	William son of Geo: Gilson buried	18
B.	Mary Watkin buried	20

Aprill 1673.

M.	John Berry & Jane Hamond married	1
B.	Thomas son of Tho: Rawson buried	8

Aprill.

B.	Richard Hall buried	12
C.	Thomas son of Tho: Beardshey Christned	13
B.	Mary daughter of Geo: Atkinson buried	21
B.	Ellen Bolton buried	24

May.

B.	Matthew son of Tho: Beardshey buried	18
	Matthew Guilliam buried	25
	Anne daughter of Mʳ Hamond Christned	27

July.

Heptenstall buried	7

July 1673.

C.	Robert son of Wᵐ Gilson christned	13
C.	Mary daughter of Tho: Mewse Christned	16
B.	Isabel wife of John Hallily buried	25

August.

B.	John Hallily buried	13
B.	Charles son of Wᵐ Bispam buried	30

September.

Mary daughter of Rob't Berridge Christned	7

October.

James Butler & Sarah Birkinshey married	16

November.

B.	Ann daughter of Katharine Harrison buried	21

December.

M.	Thomas Ingland & Susan Brook married	
C.	Jane daughter of James Bramham Christned	4

January.

C.	Elizabeth daughter of Rob't Wells Christned	6
C.	Samuel son of Wᵐ Johnson Christned	18

February.

C. Lancelot son of John Althouse Christned
B. Richard Hamond buried   3
M. John Cut & Margaret Rawson married   5
B. Ann wife of Wᵐ Wilkinson buried   15
C. Thomas son of Thomas Ingland Christned
M. William Nutter & Ann Smith married
                                        W. Strode.

March 1673.

C. Joshuah son of Mʳ Edward Topham Christned
C. William son of John Berry Christned

Aprill 1674.

B. Mⁿ Ann Leppington buried
C. Wᵐ son of Robert Tate a wandering begger Christned

May.

C. Elizabeth daughter of John Erby Christned   3
B. Ann daughter of George Wells buried   12
M. Thomas Sharp & Jane Smith married

June.

M. John Tailour & Rinbury (? Kinbury) Duffield married   8
C. Ann daughter of Benjamin Spink Christn'   8
C. Robert son of Francis Ward Christned   24
B. Richard Heptenstall buried

July.

B. Edward Winteringham buried   17
C. Jane daughter of Thomas Lee Christned   19

August.

B. Edmund Eastwood buried   5

September.

Alice daughter of Wᵐ Johnson buried   13
Matthew son of Geo: Wells Christned   27

October.

Sarah Cotes buried   3
Lydia daughter of William Turner Christned   22
Abraham Tailour buried   26
                                        W. Strode.

1674.

B. Margaret daughter of Edward Lund buried   8
C. Frances daughter of Rob't Spink Christned   14
B. Francis son of Francis Waud buried   15

December.

C. Ann daughter of Benjamin Spink Christned   3
C. Joseph son of Joseph Prat Christned   13

January.

Elizabeth daughter of Geo : Illingworth Christn.   10
Elizabeth daughter of John Erby buried   11

Richard son of Joseph Nelson Christned   20
Sarah (?) daughter of Ann Guilliam buried   21
Richard son of Joseph Nelson buried   22
.... daughter of Peter Bell Christned   26

February.

James son of Tho: Robinson Christned   9
.... son of Tho: Robinson buried   13
Mr Thomas Leppington buried   15

March.

Abraham son of Abraham Sturdy buried   7

Aprill 1675.

John son of Thomas West Christned   18
Susan daughter of William Wilkinson buried   2 (?)

May.

George son of Geo: Illingworth buried   1
William son of Wm Johnson Christned   7
Elizabeth daughter of Wm Wells Christned   30

June.

Wm Gilson buried.

June 1675.

Jane daughter of John Bustard buried.
Margaret daughter of Wm Nutter Christned.   15
Wm Smith & Jane Hall married.
Wm Brasia & Mary Whitely married   22

July.

Elizabeth wife of Thomas Meuse buried.

August.

Alice Hilham buried.
James son of Richard Oldfield Christned.

September.

Robert Empson buried.
Wm Proctor & Mary Hagur married.
Thomas son of John Vince Christned.   19

October.

Thomas son of John Wood Christned.
Jane Graves buried.

November.

Richard Harbett & Margaret Haton married   23
{ Ann daughter of William [Richard is
    erased in Register] Rily   } Christned 25
{ Elizabeth daughter of James Bramham }
Frances daughter of Geo: Laverack Christned.   28

January.

Thomas son of Wm Wilkinson Christned.   4
W^m son of John Althouse Christned
Ann daughter of Tho: Beardshey Christned   30

February.

B. Elizabeth daughter of Geo: Illingworth buried 29.

March.

Elizabeth daughter of John Flint Christned.   12
                        W. Strode.

March 1675.

C. Benjamin son of Benjamin Spink Christned.
B. William son of Wᵐ Johnson buried.

Aprill 1676.

C. Richard son of Henry Fowler Christned.
Margaret wife of John Gautris buried.
Ann daughter of Marmaduke Lund Christned.
C. Frances daughter of John Cut Christned.

May.

Ellen (?) wife of Mr Wᵐ Collinson buried   8
Margaret Turner buried   29

July.

C. Mary daughter of Thomas Dicken Christned   12
Robert Bewly & Margaret Brown married   16
Mary daughter of Anthony Heptenstall buried.   22
M. Thomas Meuse & Mary Norman married.

August.

M. George Ward & Ann Guilliam married.
M. Wᵐ Harrison & Alice Cockill married.

September.

B. {kinbury wife / John son} of John Tailor buried.

October.

C. {John son of John Bury / Ann daughter of George Gilson} Christned.
M. Robert Cockill & Margaret Moody married.
                        W. Strode.

November 1676, 1677.

Elizabeth daughter of Rob't Berridge Christned.
M. John Gawtris & Ann Addiman married.   30

December.

B. John Gilson buried.   9

January.

M. Thomas Sharp & Mercy Shillito married.
M. William Bispam & Eliz: Leatham married.
Elizabeth Bolton buried.
.... Topliff buried.
B. Thomas son of John Vince buried.
C. John son of Thomas Robinson Christned.
C. Margaret daughter of Thomas Jenkinson Christ.

February.

Thomas son of Edward Shackleton Christned.
Hugh Revell buried.

March.

Henry son of William Brasia.
Thomas Harrison buried   16

Aprill.

Richard Poole & Ellen Lund married   17
Richard Turner buried   ead.
George son of Richard Harbott Christned   20
John son of Thomas Ingland Christned   29
    [The John has been erased and Thomas written above.]
John son of John Vince Christned   29

May.

George son of George Laverack buried   18
John son of Thomas Meuse Christned   20

June.

John Machan & Elizabeth Benton married.
Ann daughter of Wᵐ Wells Christned.
       W. Strode.

1677.

Joseph son of Joseph Prat buried.   2

July.

Mʳ John Poole Schoolmaster buried.   7
Sarah daughter of Rob't Halliley buried.   23
Elizabeth daughter of Jane Bramham of Burton buried.   30

August.

. . . . daughter of James Bramham Christned.
. . . . Laverack buried.

September.

. . . . son of Benjamin Spink Christned   19

October.

Elizabeth wife of Wᵐ Bispam buried.   3
. . . . of John Gautris Christned   7
Elizabeth daughter of Wᵐ Makn (?) Christned.   7

December.

George son of Geo: Ward Christned.
Deborah daughter of Wᵐ Nutter Christned.
Margaret Sawer buried.

January.

Sarah daughter of Peter Bell Christned.

February.

John son of John Flint Christned.
Elizabeth daughter of William Procter Christned.
Jane daughter of George Wells Christned.

March.

Edward son of Marmaduke Lund Christned.
Richard son of Henry Fowler buried.

17

March 1677.

B.   Thomas son of Henry Fowler buried.

Aprill 1678.

Mary daughter of Jane Althouse Christned.
Edward Shackleton buried.

May.

Deborah daughter of Wm Rily Christned   19

June.

George Bocock & Margaret Harrison married.

C.   Margaret | Daughters of Thomas West Christned.   10
     & Mary |
C.   Joseph son of Benjamin Spink Christned.   19
B.   Mary daughter of Thomas West buried   19
C.   Jervase son of Joseph Prat Christned   30

July.

Thomas son of Edward Shackleton buried   4
Henry son of Isabel Bramfoot Christned   7
Gabriel (?) Rily & Mary Shackleton married   16
Lucy daughter of Thomas Firth Christned   27

August.

James (?) Rawson son of Margaret Cut buried   1

September.

Charles son of Robert Spink Christned   1
John (?) Berry buried   29

October.

W^m son of Wm Brasia Buried.
                                      W. Strode.

Hughe (?) son of Benjamin Spink.

November.

B.   Jane daughter of Hen Fowler buried.
     Booth son of Mr Nicolas Mauliverer Christned (?).

December.

Booth son of Mr Nicolas Mauliverer buried.
Edward Walker buried.

January.

B.   Frances Bell widow buried.
     Lancelot Bew buried.
C.   Thomas posthumous son of John Berry Christned.
B.   Isobel Gilson buried.
     Ann daughter of Jane Bramham buried.

February.

B.   Margaret daughter of Tho: West buried.

March.

     Ann wife of John Erby buried.
B.   Wm Midleton buried.
M.   Wm Applegarth & Sarah Parnham married.
     Thomas England buried.
     Ann daughter of George Bocock Christned.
C.   .... son of .... Cut Christned (?)
     Isobel Bramfoot.

INDEX OF NAMES.

Beadshay, Beardshay, Beardshey, Bear-
shey:
———, Thomas, 108, 112, 113, 114,
117, 125, 127.
Beale, Elizabeth, 116, 119.
——, Frances, 119.
——, John, 115, 116, 119.
Beatson, Ann, 124.
——, Ellen, 124.
Beamond, Ursula, 34.
Becket, Richary, 47.
——, Roger, 47.
———, ... 29.
Bedforth, James, 106.
Bedall, Beedall:
——, Fraunces, 51.
——, John, 48, 51, 52, 53, 54.
——, Margaret, 48.
——, Maria, 51.
——, Mary, 53.
Behowse, Katteren, 10.
Belhowse, An, 9.
Bell, Anne, 92.
——, Elizabeth, 124.
——, Frances, 130.
——, George, 117.
——, Isabel, 121.
——, Jane, 92.
——, John, 92.
——, Katharin, 96.
——, Michael, 121.
——, Peter, 113, 117, 121, 122, 124, 127,
129.
——, Thomas, 113.
——, William, 74, 78, 92.
Bellabee, Bellabie, Bellaby, Bellobee:
———, Anne, 91.
———, Christopher, 46.
———, Jennet, 74.
———, John, 5, 6.
———, William, 42, 74, 77, 82.
Belton, Margaret, 49.
Benbow, Ann, 63.
——, Jenet, 50.
——, Robert, 42.
Benet, Bennet:
——, Jenet, 16.
——, Robert, 15, 16.
Benige, Jenet, 19.
Bennetland, Jenet, 64.
Benson, Anne, 100.
———, Laurence, 94.
———, Walter, 98, 100.
Benton, Elizabeth, 129.
Berkinshey, Birkinshey:
——— ——, Esther, 115.
——— ——, John, 117.
——— — —, Mathew, 115, 117, 124.
——— ——, Sarah, 125.

Beredge, Beridge, Berredge, Berridge,
Birridge:
——, Agnes, 39.
——, Alice, 2, 32, 46, 48, 117.
——, An or Anne, 4, 74, 90, 112.
——, Cicilie, 53.
——, Dorithie or Dorothy, 51, 121.
——, Elizabethe, 27, 88, 128.
——, Ellyn, 53.
——, Ester, 96.
——, George, 37, 38.
——, Isabell, 8, 44.
——, Jane, 41, 73.
——, Jenet, 1, 8, 24.
——, John, 37, 42, 53, 90, 121.
——, Margaret, 28.
——, Mary, 46, 48, 71, 82, 125.
——, Nicholas, 50, 53.
——, Richard, 32, 35.
——, Robert, 17, 35, 37, 39, 42, 44,
48, 50, 51, 52, 53, 77, 82, 88,
90, 107, 108, 110, 112, 115,
117, 121, 123, 125, 128.
——, Thomas, 44, 53.
——, Widow, 46.
——, William, 14, 17, 19, 27, 28, 32,
33, 37, 38, 40, 41, 43, 45, 115.
Beregh, Jenet, 5.
Beree, Berre, Berree, Berrie, Berry,
Bery:
——, An or Anne, 77, 105.
——, Beatrix, 61.
——, Elizabeth, 63, 97, 99, 109.
——, Jane, 71, 103.
——, Jennett, 97.
——, Joan, 89.
——, John, 57, 58, 61, 63, 66, 71, 86,
87, 88, 92, 97, 99, 101, 102,
105, 109, 110, 125, 126, 128,
130.
——, Katharin, 88.
——, Mary, 69.
——, Rebecha, 92.
——, Sarah, 101, 105.
——, Thomas, 61, 66, 87, 130.
——, William, 61, 98, 99, 101, 126.
Berwick, Ann, 118.
——, Elizabeth, 115.
——, William, 115, 118, 122.
Bew, Bewe, Beaw, Beawe:
——, Agnes, 62.
——, Alice, 30, 35, 119, 123.
——, An or Ann, 66, 100, 118, 122.
——, Elizabeth, 116, 123, 124.
——, George, 42, 72, 73, 74, 75, 78, 81,
85, 88, 98, 100, 101, 105, 108,
112, 113, 115, 118, 120, 123, 124.
——, Jane, 88, 121, 122, 123.

G.

Scrivener, Elizabeth, 10, 18, 39.
———, Fraunces, 31, 33, 34, 37, 39, 41, 45, 47, 50.
———, Hellen, 55.
———, Jenet, 38.
———, John, 7, 18, 19.
———, Katteren, 8, 18.
———, Margaret, 37.
———, Ralph, 23.
———, William, 33.
Scroop, Margaret, 48.
Scroope, An, 48.
Sedall, Elizabethe, 68.
———, Vincent, 68.
Selbee, Sellby:
———, Brian, 58.
———, George, 58, 60, 85, 87.
———, Jane, 60.
———, Sibella, 60, 85.
———, Urseley, 89.
Settle, Margaret, 113.
Shackleton, Edward, 129, 130.
———, Mary, 130.
———, Thomas, 129, 130.
Shan, Anne, 50, 53.
———, Elizabeth, 110.
———, Robert, 46, 47, 50, 53, 54.
———, Thomas, 53, 54.
Sharp, Edward, 60.
———, John, 54, 55, 57, 65, 66.
———, Leonard, 65.
———, Marie, 65.
———, Thomas, 60, 126, 128.
———, William, 54.
Sharphowse, William, 45.
Sharpulls, Agnes, 15.
Shaw, Shawe:
———, Elizabeth, 70.
———, George, 73, 99, 107.
———, Marget, 77, 105, 109.
———, Mary, 84, 86.
———, Richard, 69.
———, Susan, 80.
———, William, 69, 70, 73, 77, 80, 84, 86, 99, 105, 107, 112.
Shepherd, Sheaperd, Shepperd, Shipperd, Shypherd, Shyppherd:
———, Alice, 14.
———, An, 18.
———, Isabell, 11.
———, John, 9.
———, Margaret, 7, 28.
———, Richard, 95.
———, Robert, 13, 14.
———, Thomas, 14, 17, 18.
Shereburn, Thomas, 34, 46.
Shereburne, Margaret, 72.
Sherecroft, Alice, 66.

Sherecroft, Christopher, 65.
———, Richard, 100.
———, William, 66.
———, Xpofer, 66.
Shereing, Mary, 103.
Shillito, Ann, 99.
———, John, 95, 97.
———, Mercy, 128.
———, Thomas, 97.
Shippen, Shipen:
———, Alexander, 40.
———, Alice, 5.
———, An, 11, 34, 39.
———, Dorithie, 18, 35.
———, Edward, 21.
———, Fraunces, 21, 30, 31.
———, Isabell, 3, 9.
———, James, 9, 27, 30, 32, 34, 35, 37.
———, Jane, 32.
———, Jenet, 2, 13.
———, John, 6, 11, 17, 18, 21, 30, 31, 33, 34, 69, 75.
———, Margaret, 6, 51, 69.
———, Martyn, 24.
———, Mary, 27, 73.
———, Richard, 53, 75.
———, Robert, 2.
———, Thomas, 3, 5, 30, 33.
———, William, 8, 53, 56, 73.
———, ..., 22.
Short, Alice, 70.
———, Anna, 98.
———, John, 70.
———, Mary, 95.
Siddall, Vincent, 77, 81.
Sikes, Sykes:
———, John, 2, 3, 13.
———, Marie, 108.
———, Richard, 108, 110, 116.
———, William, 116.
Simpson, Simson, Sympson, Symson:
———, Alice, 10, 35, 89.
———, An, 76, 83.
———, Dorithy, 29.
———, Elizabeth, 24.
———, Jenet, 6.
———, John, 12, 25, 32.
———, Thomas, 58.
———, William, 5, 8, 18, 54, 67, 97.
Simpull, John, 2.
Skelton, Ellin, 94.
———, Helling, 110.
———, William, 98.
Skilbeck, Skilbecke:
———, Barbara, 37, 38.
———, Elizabeth, 30.
———, John, 30, 32, 33, 37, 38.
———, Katteren, 38.

Skilbeck, Robert, 19.
Slillitson, Dynnys, 56.
Smawlechar, Edmund, 17.
————, John, 17.
Smith, Smithe, Smyth, Smythe:
——, Agnes, 30.
——, Ann, 12, 43, 44, 45, 85, 93, 115, 126.
——, Charles, 88, 93, 97, 103, 109, 118.
——, Dorithie, 32.
——, Duke, 93.
——, Elizabeth, 106, 109.
——, Fraunces, 8, 25, 94.
——, George, 44.
——, James, 113, 117, 119.
——, Jane, 97, 126.
——, Jenet, 6, 9, 13, 45, 51.
——, John, 3, 5, 12, 13, 44, 51.
——, Katteren, 26.
——, Leonard, 87.
——, Margaret, 3, 20, 41, 82, 107.
——, Mary, 102.
——, Richard, 24, 45, 102, 106.
——, Robert, 8.
——, Roger, 40.
——, Thomas, 5, 6, 10, 26, 31, 49, 71, 94, 98.
——, William, 10, 38, 40, 41, 88, 96, 98, 107, 109, 110, 113, 117, 119, 122, 127.
Smithies, Smythies:
————, Edithe, 52.
————, Elizabeth, 52.
————, George, 38, 52.
————, Henry, 57.
————, Idethe, 54.
————, Isabell, 58.
————, Thomas, 38.
Snawden, Agnes, 47.
————, Isabell, 58.
Snawesden, Isabell, 79.
Snawsdell, Snawesdall, Snawesdayll, Snawsdayl:
————, Arcillas, 89.
————, Christopher, 56.
————, Elizabeth, 86.
————, Hercules, 91.
————, Jane, 91.
————, Margrit, 89.
Sommers, Julian, 93.
————, Robert, 93.
Sommersell, Godfry, 95.
————, John, 95.
Sowersby, John, 19.
Spencer, Spenser:
————, Margaret, 22.
————, Mary, 21.
————, William, 20.

Spicer, Spiser:
————, Agnes, 45.
————, Anne, 65.
————, Hughe, 19.
Spink, Spinck, Spincke, Spinke, Spynck:
——, Alice, 16, 47, 59.
——, An, 20, 53, 83, 88, 101, 104, 107, 109, 111, 112, 114, 126.
——, Auvaray, 88.
——, Benjamin, 93, 120, 121, 122, 124, 126, 128, 129, 130.
——, Charles, 130.
——, Christopher, 87, 110, 111.
——, Dorothie, 91, 115.
——, Elizabeth, 42, 46, 48, 62, 68, 78, 101, 111, 117, 123.
——, Francis, 126.
——, Gabriell, 124.
——, George, 49, 57, 59, 76, 78, 81, 83, 86, 89, 90, 91, 94, 119, 120.
——, Godfrey, 50, 83, 84, 88, 90, 93, 106.
——, Hughe, 130.
——, James, 54.
——, Jane, 117, 119, 120.
——, John, 41, 42, 43, 44, 46, 47, 48, 50, 51, 53, 54, 56, 57, 59, 68, 78, 102, 105, 107, 111, 112, 114, 116, 117, 120, 121, 122, 123.
——, Joseph, 93, 130.
——, Katherine, 84, 120.
——, Margaret, 18, 36, 51.
——, Mathias, 89, 119.
——, Omphray, 107.
——, Posthumus, 110, 111, 115.
——, Rebeca, 89.
——, Richard, 59.
——, Robert, 15, 43, 44, 47, 49, 52, 56, 59, 60, 85, 86, 115, 116, 117, 119, 120, 121, 122, 123, 124, 130.
——, Ruth, 122.
——, Sarah, 92, 93.
——, Thomas, 15, 16, 18, 20, 22, 26, 33, 44, 56, 78, 80, 83, 85, 88, 89, 92, 93, 107, 109, 115, 117, 120, 121, 126.
——, William, 46, 56, 116.
——, Xpofer, 47, 87.
Splayforth, Alice, 113.
————, Edward, 116.
————, Henry, 110, 111, 113, 116.
————, Marie, 111.
Spoffard, Spofforth, Spoforth, Spofourth:
————, Agnes, 25.
————, Alce, 91.
————, An, 19.
————, Richard, 50.
Staffurth, Alice, 6.
Stainton, Jenet, 4, 5.

——, Katherin, 99.
——, Robert, 93, 96, 99, 105.
——, Thomas, 27, 30.

Y.

YEADON, Yeaden:
——, Alice, 37, 39, 66.
——, Isabell, 73.
——, John, 37, 39, 45.

Youle, Yoyle:
——, Alice, 18.
——, An, 14.
——, John, 2.
——, Robert, 14.
Young, Younge:
——, An, 13.
——, Fraunces, 6, 9.
——, Henry, 4, 22.
——, Margaret, 7.

INDEX OF PLACES.

ADDINGHAM, 51, 60.
BARSTOW, 103.
Barton, 109.
Beal, 29.
Bettrice hil, 66.
Bigging, 103.
Birkin, 27, 30, 59.
Blithe, 42.
Boltan Poirrie, 108.
Braton or Brayton, 16, 45, 48, 102, 104.
Brighton, 45.
Brotherton, 77, 79.
Burton, 14, 15, 16, 17, 18, 19, 20, 21, 26, 27, 28, 38, 39, 40, 41, 43, 45, 46, 47, 48, 49, 50, 51, 52, 53, 54, 55, 56, 57, 58, 60, 61, 65, 67, 72, 74, 77, 102, 103, 104, 109, 113, 114, 123, 129.
Burton Salmon, 55, 104.
COATES, 52.
DARBYSHIRE, 74.
Dranfeild, 74.
Duffield, 126.
FENTON, 103.
Frieston or Friston, 13, 14, 15, 16, 17, 19, 20, 21, 26, 27, 29, 38, 48, 49, 50, 51, 52, 53, 54, 55, 56, 59, 61, 67, 100.
Frieston Ings, 74.
GATEFORTH, 47, 102, 104.
Gilling, 49.
Guyseley, 52.
HAMBLETON, 45, 48, 55.
Hemsworth, 122.
Heslewood, 66.
Hilham, Hillam, Hillom, Hillome, or Hyllam, 13, 14, 15, 16, 17, 18, 19, 20, 21, 27, 28, 29, 31, 32, 33, 35, 36, 37, 43, 47, 48, 49, 50, 51, 52, 53, 54, 55, 56, 57, 58, 62, 66, 73, 83, 87, 100, 101, 102, 103, 104, 108, 109, 110, 113, 121.
Hurst Courtney, 59.
KELLINGTON, 100.
Kippax, 103.
LANCASHIRE, 76.
Ledsam or Ledsham, 103, 104, 109.
Leeds, 29, 37, 39.
Lennarton, 76.
Lodingde, 14.
London, 51.
Lumbe, Lumbee, Lumbie, or Lumby, 19, 25, 34, 52, 63, 65, 66, 67, 69, 71, 73, 74, 76, 77, 79, 100, 101, 111.
Lumby layne, 53.
MELTAN LEYES, 109.
Milford, Milfoord, Milfoorth, Milforth, Millfoorthe, or Mylford, 14, 65, 67, 69, 70, 73, 75, 100, 106, 114, 122.
Monckfrieston or Monckfriston, 1, 14, 15, 16, 17, 18, 19, 49, 52, 64, 78, 102, 103, 104, 108, 112.
NEWCASTLE, 73.
North Cowton, 77.
OLDAM, 76.
POMFRET, 65.
Pontefract, 104.
RAWDEN, 52.
Rest Parke, 102, 103.
Ripon, 63.
SAXTON, 104.
Scotton, 104.
Shearburne, Sherburn, Shereburn, Shereburne, or Shirburne, 13, 14, 15, 16, 49, 52, 66, 102, 103, 104, 110.
South Milfoord, South Milford, or South Milforth, 62, 65, 66, 70, 76.
Steeton, 49.
Stillingfleet, 41, 44.
Susworth, 104.
Swillington, 16.
TANCHILL, Tanshelfe, or Tanshill, 102, 103, 104.
WAKEFEILD, 105.
Wauldbee, 73.
Winde Milne, 64.
Wistow or Wistowe, 64, 66, 112.
Woodhowse, 14.
YORK or Yorke, 36, 107.

ROBERT WHITE, ANTIQUARIAN AND GENEALOGICAL PRINTER, WORKSOP.

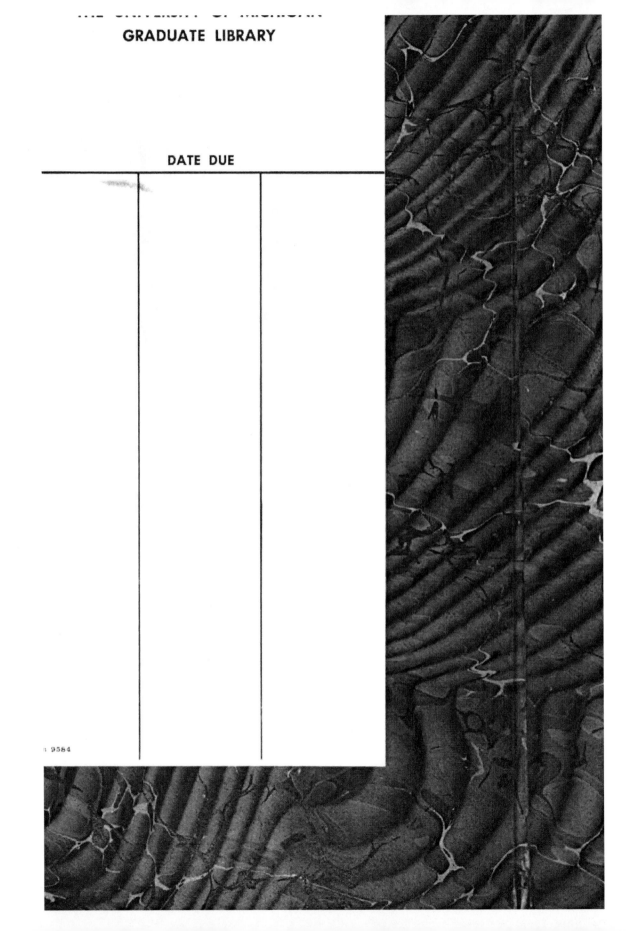

CPSIA information can be obtained at www.ICGtesting.com

229404LV00003B/23/P

9 781148 559582